MW00586341

MATH MIND

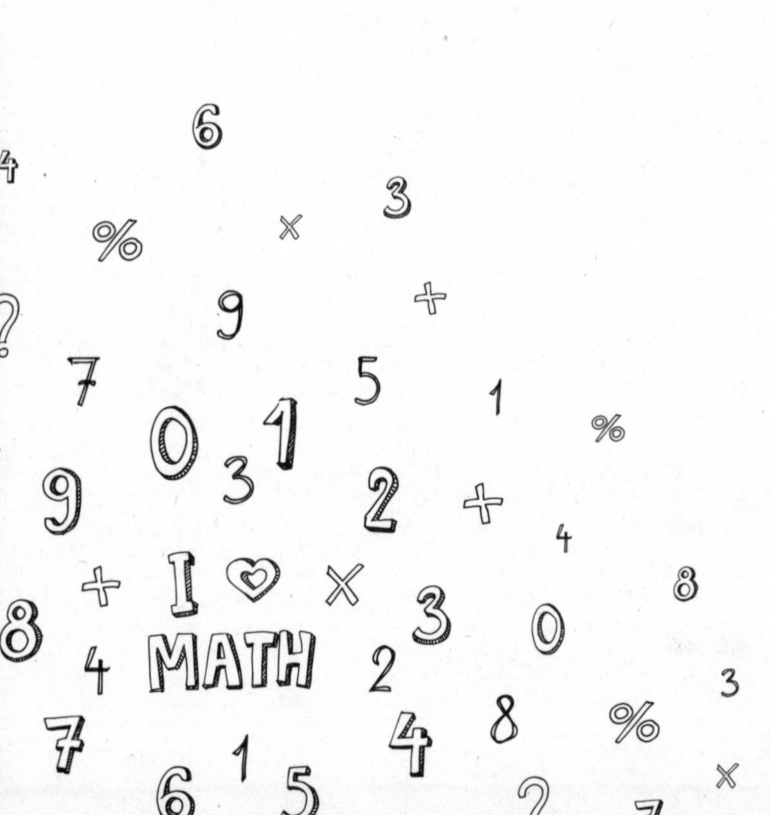
I
MATH

Math Mind

THE SIMPLE PATH TO LOVING MATH

Shalinee Sharma

Avery
an imprint of Penguin Random House
New York

an imprint of Penguin Random House LLC
penguinrandomhouse.com

Most Avery books are available at special quantity discounts for bulk purchase for sales promotions, premiums, fundraising, and educational needs. Special books or book excerpts also can be created to fit specific needs. For details, write SpecialMarkets@ penguinrandomhouse.com.

Library of Congress Cataloging-in-Publication Data

Names: Sharma, Shalinee, author.
Title: Math mind: the simple path to loving math / Shalinee Sharma.
Description: New York: Avery, an imprint of Penguin Random House, [2024] | Includes index.
Identifiers: LCCN 2023044481 (print) | LCCN 2023044482 (ebook) |
ISBN 9780593543504 (hardcover) | ISBN 9780593543528 (epub)
Subjects: LCSH: Mathematics—Popular works.
Classification: LCC QA93.S458 2024 (print) | LCC QA93 (ebook) |
DDC 510—dc23/eng/20240314
LC record available at https://lccn.loc.gov/2023044481
LC ebook record available at https://lccn.loc.gov/2023044482

Printed in the United States of America
1st Printing

Illustrations by Cat Haung

Book design by Shannon Nicole Plunkett

To all my teachers who taught me to love learning,
and especially to my two most important
teachers, my mom and dad, who always
encouraged me to try my best.

Contents

AUTHOR'S NOTE: The stories in this book reflect the author's recollection of events. Some names, locations, and identifying characteristics have been changed to protect the privacy of those depicted. Dialogue has been re-created from memory.

Introduction

The first thing you should know about me is that I am not a math prodigy. But in sixth grade, I transferred schools and was unexpectedly placed in honors math. I got lost on my way to class, and when I walked in late, I found something I had never seen before: a classroom of confident, happy boys bouncing around in the front, with a few girls quietly sitting in the back. I knew where I belonged, but the only seat left was in the front row. For the first few weeks, I silently identified with the girls in the back—cowed, self-doubting, and never raising their hands.

After our first test, Mr. Snyder said, "You did well. If you try your very best, you could be just as good as the boys." It was a terrible thing to say by today's standards, but it rocked my middle school world. I knew I was behind where I needed to be, but I heard Mr. Snyder's inspiring message: If I worked hard, I could not only catch up, but I could compete with the best.

It changed my self-expectations. I had already unconsciously decided that I was just lucky to be in the room and that I would spend the year hanging on for dear life. Mr. Snyder told me that I belonged in that room and that if I made the effort, I could thrive.

With that emboldening knowledge, I did work hard. In that hard work, I found the beauty and pleasure of math itself—not the relief of doing well on a test, not the reward of pleasing others, but the plain sensation of enjoyment when solving a puzzle, when finding a path to everything making sense. I was pleased as ratios fell into place on a ratio table, and I felt the intense "Aha!" moment of understanding that y does in fact equal $mx + b$ when I plotted points on the coordinate plane. I was learning not just to do math but to love math.

I didn't do it alone. My father jumped in as my math tutor, and my mother as my unwavering cheerleader. My father loved math, which had altered the trajectory of his life, allowing him to transcend the wreckage of the refugee crisis caused by the Partition of India to a comfortable life as a physician in the United States. My mother, also a refugee of Partition and a physician, is happiest when working hard. She knew that hard work needed high-quality fuel and that I would eat more fruit if she cut it into fun shapes. I became one of the math kids—I wasn't born one, but I discovered that I could transform myself into one.

That discovery has made all the difference in my life, and it can make all the difference in yours, too. I've seen numeracy change people's lives for the better, many millions of times over. With a team of amazing teachers and technologists, I have built a nonprofit called Zearn, the top-rated math learning platform for elementary and middle school children, which includes free digital lessons for every day of kindergarten through eighth grade.

I'm far from the first person to praise the virtues of math. The word *mathematics* comes from the Latin root word meaning "to learn." Mathematics has been at the center of every recorded human civilization. The groundbreaking ideas formulated thousands of years ago by Mesopotamian, Egyptian, Chinese, Indian, Mayan, and Greek mathematicians continue to shape human destiny every day as we use them for both the most mundane and cerebral tasks. From the basic concept of zero to the advanced idea of a differential, math is at the center of human history. Math illuminates the structures that create beauty and wonder in music, architecture, and art.

But most kids hate math, and what they are taught is that math hates them back. Implicitly rather than explicitly, our way of teaching communicates to the majority of students that they don't have what it takes to be good at math. Being good at math, as we teach it, means memorizing multiplication tables and tedious algorithms. We reward students who shout out correct answers the fastest. We teach to the multiple-choice test. In doing so, we make math rote, high-stakes, and scary. And for those who don't thrive, we comfort them with the bromide that seals their fate: "Don't worry, you are a creative type; *math just isn't your thing.*"

How did something so essential to humanity become so out of reach? Math belongs to all of us, but so many of us have lost touch with it. Imagine if schools sent the same message about reading: "Some of you are natural readers, but most of you just don't have the literacy gene, so don't worry, books are going the way of the dinosaur anyway." I'm constantly hearing "We don't need to teach all this math; we have computers and calculators to do it for us." Do we not need to learn to read because Alexa can read to us?

I first started thinking about writing this book on one cold February day when the negativity around math became too much for me. I was waiting to pick up my kids from preschool, lost in my thoughts—work-related minutiae, self-scolding for being late to pickup, a gathering sense of doom over my lack of physical fitness and the fourth-floor walk-up to the Montessori classroom—when another parent started talking.

"She's like me, basically," the woman said. "She's just not a math kid."

I looked up, alarmed and disoriented, trying to hide my emotions. This mom was talking about a preschooler, whose education had barely begun. And already she was ruling out an entire world of knowledge.

"You know?" she continued. "She's just not a math-y type. She loves her letters, though. We are, you know, creative types."

As usual, for the good of our family, I did my best to fake

being a normal person, one who does not work in math education. I could not quickly think of how to let her know how dead wrong she was and still leave an opening that my kids could be invited for playdates. Seconds later, our children filed out of the classroom. Her ebullient little girl ran into her arms full-force, knocking her back a bit.

"Basically, your boys are math kids," the woman said. "We are just not math people."

The blood rushed to my brain, my heart pounding in my head. I wanted to scream: *She can hear you. She may even remember this. Please. Stop. Talking.*

As we walked down the four flights of stairs together, I found my words, though I shared them quietly. "Your daughter is a math person," I said. "So are you. Math is creative and beautiful."

She gave me a wry, curious smile, and I knew she didn't believe me.

The very morning of that ill-fated pickup, I was reading in a coffee shop and got into an unwanted conversation with a stranger. The woman asked me what I did, and I said that I create math learning experiences for kids and teachers, to help all kids love math. She stared into my eyes intensely, paused, and said: "Math terrified me all through middle and high school. I beat it, though. I only strongly dislike it now. I guess I do use it every day, though, when I put budgets together at work."

Right before this encounter, I had been peacefully sipping

a cappuccino and reading a bestselling book about cultivating creativity and noncomformist paths through life. And there in the first chapter, the author was disparaging math and questioning the value of algebra as a literary device to make his broader point.

Three different ways, on that single Tuesday in February, math was being disparaged, feared, or reviled around me. I knew something had to change and that we have the power to change it. When we change the narrative, and change our attitudes, math will be something we all see as our own.

We can restore math to its central role in our lives and our civilization. In these pages, I'll argue for a new math mentality in three sections. The first focuses on three myths that prevent kids from embracing math in ways that develop their math brains. The second part of the book identifies the specific methods we can use to learn math better—so that kids (and adults) learn to love it rather than learn to hate or avoid it. The third section addresses the roadblocks to achieving this vision and makes the case that numeracy is essential to achieving the future we all desire.

In this last section, as well as throughout, I'll describe the benefits of widespread numeracy—not just for society but for individual success and satisfaction. The motivation for parents to help their kids become facile with numbers is obvious—it can help them become more successful adults. But let's start with the six key benefits for everyone:

1. Mastering problem-solving skills
2. Developing a reasoning mind
3. Creating more career choices and opportunities
4. Learning the language of personal finance
5. Working and participating to the fullest in the digital world
6. Soothing the soul

This last benefit requires a bit of explanation. Contrary to common belief, math is not a dry, dull exercise. Instead, it has much in common with art. When people give themselves over to math—when they're willing to explore it freely and creatively—they experience a sense of wonder. In a stress-filled, volatile universe, kids and adults need this more than ever before. Kids whose souls are soothed by math grow up open to and appreciative of the elegance of its constructs. They are comforted by the logic of equations and find beauty in how everything from the shape of our galaxy to the rhythms of music adheres to mathematical models.

This notion of the glories of math may run counter to your experience. You may be saying to yourself, “She is talking about other people, not me.” Or: “She’s talking about other kids, not my kid.” In fact, I’m talking about you. I am talking about everyone, as the next chapter will make clear. We all could have been math kids. Now we all have the potential to be math people.

CHAPTER 1

We All Could Have Been Math Kids

WHAT IF I TOLD YOU THAT WE DON'T REALLY KNOW much about how we learn math?

For all the rigid rules and drills in the classroom, behind the scenes there's a shocking lack of certainty. "What do we really know about how to teach math to children?" the writer Jay Caspian Kang asked in a recent article on the state of math education. "The answer is not all that much—and what little we do know is highly contested."

This is a startling thing to hear about one of the fundamental building blocks of K–12 learning. Especially considering that an understanding of fractions in elementary school predicts the completion of algebra, and completion of algebra is the most predictive activity in K–12 of getting to and through college. Math can change life trajectories.

But what Kang found is also what I have found on my own more than decade-long journey through math education. In building and constantly improving a K–8 math learning platform, which now serves millions of students and hundreds of thousands of teachers, I've witnessed up close how much doubt and disagreement there is about basic questions of how to build mathematical minds.

More than a decade in, however, I know one thing for certain. We all could have been math kids.

Ten years ago, I wouldn't have believed it. While I knew I *became* a math kid and wasn't simply born one, I had not generalized my experience. But various events, especially the COVID period, took me on a high-intensity learning journey. As an optimist, I'd like to have believed in everyone's innate ability. But I am a skeptical optimist, meaning that I can believe something only when I see it with my own eyes. I assumed my personal experience was a one-off and that math success was a rare inborn ability, because that's the dominant societal narrative. Though I had worked hard and scraped by, I still assumed that the majority who succeeded with math were those with natural abilities.

Why does what we believe about math learning matter? Because the assumptions we start with matter, and some even decide the outcome. Assumptions consciously and unconsciously shape our behavior. Right out of college, I had a job where I built financial models that attempted to predict outcomes. As part of our training, we were told it was essential to find and explore our most sensitive assumption in the analytical model, meaning the variable that, if changed, would totally change the outcome or the answer the model would point us to.

Sitting alone late at night in my cubicle with my Excel spreadsheets, finding the most sensitive assumption, I would get lost in thought, dwelling on what assumptions were most sensitive in other parts of my life. If I want to drink better coffee and eat authentic Indian food, could I assume the cafés and Indian restaurants would improve in Boston? If not, then should I move? These assumptions can predict the future because inadvertently, they can decide the future.

Consider that "Who can learn math?" and "How do we teach math?" are two fundamentally divergent questions. Each starts from a radically different assumption and goes on to manifest itself distinctly. In one project we are sorting, and in the other we are teaching.

To grasp the importance of assumptions about who can learn math, let me share the untold story of the American high school revolution. In 1890, fewer than 7 percent of American students went to high school. High school was a luxury for the rich or a privilege for those who could pass an admissions test. All enjoying this luxury were born the right gender and ethnicity. Yet by 1940, the share of US children attending high school had risen more than tenfold to over 70 percent. This dramatic change in the way America chose to educate its children transformed the culture, economy, and politics of the twentieth and twenty-first centuries and was seminal to the American-led global technology revolution that we are still in today.

It's hard to overstate how seismic this shift was. Historically in the United States and Europe, children were tested (read "sorted") by the specific high school they sought to attend, to determine if they were worthy. In the first decade of the twentieth century, America checked that sorting-based assumption. The zeitgeist shifted suddenly and many education leaders began to wonder if the act of going to high school would enable students to do well on the kind of tasks the admissions tests were assessing for and thus become more productive members of society.

Horace Mann, an education leader from the early 1800s who didn't live to see the high school revolution but influenced its design, advocated for free and universal education. He wrote that education "is a great equalizer of conditions of men—the balance wheel of the social machinery." While Europe continued to sort and test, the US decided to teach "everyone," including girls. (However, in most places "everyone" still included only those who were white. The work of integrating our education system continues today.) With this investment in children, in our human capital, the United States surpassed other developed countries at the time in technological and economic advancement. It turned out it *was* better for everyone to teach all students a high school curriculum instead of just the chosen few. Within a few decades, Europe followed suit. The American high school revolution, not the European sorting model, became our default setting for all countries across the world.

Positive Deviance

Let me circle back to the first experience that pushed me to question my assumptions. In 2012, I had quit my fast-paced job in business to start the nonprofit Zearn with a group of educators. Though I had spent more than a decade in business, I had never planned to be in the industry that long. As a child, I told people that I wanted to work at the American Red Cross, though I did not know what that meant. In college, I explored careers in the social sector and direct service. Among the ways I wanted to serve, education held a special place.

As the child of refugees, I had seen firsthand how access to an excellent education could transform lives. Once, both of my parents had been small children on the wrong side of the border. In the summer of 1947, as India won its independence from colonial rule, the devastating and hastily planned Partition by the British—with India and Pakistan on each side of a new border—resulted in the displacement of fourteen million people and an estimated three million deaths. It's the largest refugee crisis in human history. As a child, watching the aftershocks of Partition unfold in my family on multiple continents, I learned three key lessons: how an education could change the trajectory of a life, how many people weren't sufficiently lucky to obtain one, and how grossly unfair the whole system was. So, when the chance to spend my time and energy increasing access to education emerged, I grabbed it.

We founded Zearn to answer two questions: Could we continue the work of the high school revolution using digital tools to further democratize access to an excellent education? How could technology complement the work of teaching and learning? While charting our path, I found that the most interesting answers were to questions I had not initially asked, and I came to question several assumptions I didn't know I had.

There was no manual for what I wanted to do. I had to go a different way. In the book *Switch*, Chip and Dan Heath share a schema for solving hard problems in the absence of existing instructions. The method is to study "bright spots," the particular cases when things go right against the odds. In rural Vietnam, they write, child malnutrition was seen as an inevitable result of poverty and poor sanitation, so that nothing could be done about it until those underlying problems were solved. In the 1990s, leaders of Save the Children in Vietnam decided that these beliefs were true but useless. They couldn't wait for poverty and unsanitary conditions to be fixed to deal with malnutrition.

The team looked at the children who were somehow thriving in the same context that left others malnourished. They identified many small, subtle parental behaviors that departed from the norm: some mothers fed their kids four times a day instead of the usual two, dividing up the same amount of food into more meals. Feeding kids by hand rather than having them eat from a communal bowl also produced healthier outcomes, as did giving them bits of shrimp and crab found in the rice paddies, which was considered inappropriate for kids, and sweet potato greens, which were regarded as a weed.

During my own pathfinding period, I began to search for bright spots. I met teachers whose students came from low-income neighborhoods and were scoring at the highest level on the annual state math tests. While, in general, wealth and resourcing are sadly too predictive of educational achievement for the health of our society, here we saw a positive deviance, remarkable success against the odds. Observing these teachers, I discovered they were employing subtle but highly effective techniques that helped their students learn and love math—doing for education what bits of shellfish and sweet potato greens did for nutrition.

Take a look at this problem:

Which fraction has a value closest to $\frac{1}{2}$?

$$\frac{5}{8} \quad \frac{1}{6} \quad \frac{2}{2} \quad \frac{1}{5}$$

You might have been taught to solve this problem the same ways I was taught. First, I would spend several minutes struggling to find a common denominator between the fractions in front of me. What is the common multiple of 8, 6, 2, and 5? After several computations, I would get to 120. I'd then work through many more computations to convert all the fractions to a new fraction with 120 as the denominator. My work would look something like this.

$$\frac{1}{2} \quad \frac{5}{8} \quad \frac{1}{6} \quad \frac{2}{2} \quad \frac{1}{5} \; \} \text{ Common denominator?}$$

$$(2) \; (2 \cdot 2 \cdot 2) \; (2 \cdot 3) \; (2) \; (5)$$

$$2 \cdot 2 \cdot 2 \cdot 3 \cdot 5 = 120$$

$$\frac{60}{120} \quad \frac{75}{120} \quad \frac{20}{120} \quad \frac{120}{120} \quad \frac{24}{120}$$

$$\frac{5}{8} \quad \frac{1}{6} \quad \frac{2}{2} \quad \frac{1}{5}$$

But some teachers I met were teaching these problems differently, creating positive deviance—just like the Vietnamese parents who were feeding their kids differently, resulting in positive health outcomes. These teachers were focused on their students' deeply understanding the math. They didn't prioritize only making them work through the procedures of finding the least common multiple, though their students could certainly compute accurately and utilize these strategies when required. They knew that kids could go through the motions and take several minutes to do dozens of calculations to come up with the answer. They also knew that students could do this accurately without the least bit of understanding of what they were doing. Finally, they knew this was a failing proposition.

When the teachers shared a problem like this, the first thing they did was to turn the fractions into meaning. They would instruct the students, "Remember fractions are numbers, not hieroglyphic symbols. Before you follow all the procedures, make sure you understand this problem. Use pictures or tell yourself a story. Do whatever you need to do."

Some teachers drew pictures like this on the board to move the fractions from symbolic gobbledygook to meaning everyone could grasp.

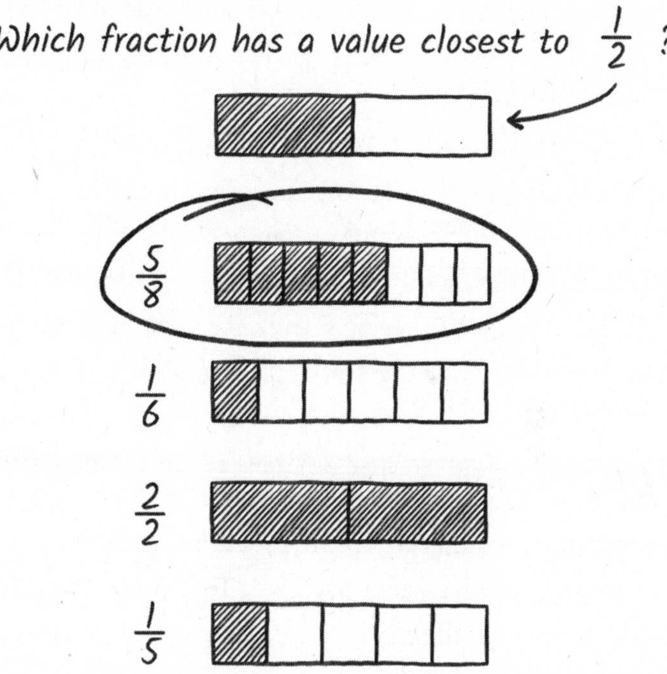

They showed their students that understanding was essential in mathematics, and sometimes the reward was having no need to calculate at all.

I was thunderstruck by this difference. Because this is what I did by myself in my sixth-grade bedroom to survive and eventually succeed in Mr. Snyder's math class. I was so far behind, I couldn't go back and memorize all the procedures and tricks I had missed, so I tried another strategy. I tried to leapfrog and understand. I now have words for what I was doing. In order to understand, I made easier problems, drew pictures, or tried another way. While sometimes it took much longer, I worked to understand rather than only memorize. And here in these classrooms I visited, kids were being shown that there was meaning. They were being taught to look for and find understanding; they were taught to expect it. It electrified me to see. No wonder these kids were succeeding. They were being taught the number sense that some of us had been lucky enough to figure out on our own.

By the way, that wasn't just any old math problem. That was a problem from the National Assessment of Educational Progress, or NAEP—an educational assessment tool given to a representative sample of fourth and eighth graders. NAEP, referred to as "the nation's report card," is the key way we know how kids are doing in math in America. On this particular question, we failed: 75 percent of American fourth graders got it wrong; 41 percent of fourth graders selected two halves or one whole as the correct answer. That is the largest number offered as a choice—and the value furthest from one-half. With the understanding those pictures offer, no student would select $\frac{2}{2}$ as a correct answer. In the positive deviance classrooms, a tedious problem of disembodied computations becomes a simpler problem of reasoning.

Building a Better Math Brain

Seeking the path to effective strategies, I needed to learn a lot about various subjects, including brain science. What I learned reinforced my belief that math kids are made, not born. In recent years, cognitive science and related fields have yielded a rich trove of knowledge that our brains aren't fixed, but are dynamic—*plasticity* is the relevant term here, describing the brain's capacity for change.

This ran counter to my understanding. I had come to think of the brain's capacity as fixed: You were smart or you were not. You were good at writing or math or you were not. I knew hard work mattered. I had worked diligently to make it through sixth grade. And I watched my parents retrain as physicians in the United States, aiming to make a fantastic life for my brother and me. But deep down, I still believed the fundamentals were fixed. Digging into the science, however, I found quite the opposite. It was astonishingly simple. The brain can get smarter in the same way that the body can get stronger. If you do push-ups every day, you will be able to do more and more push-ups. You will quickly exceed what you thought was possible for yourself and what others thought possible for you. Muscles get stronger. The brain works similarly. The brain can get smarter.

Consider the story of a little boy named Tanner from New Stanton, Pennsylvania. At age four, Tanner Collins had a golf ball–size tumor in his brain that was causing seizures. By the time he was in first grade, he was having fifty seizures a day. His doctors removed one-sixth of Tanner's brain, including the entire visual processing center on his right side. Contrary to expectations, Tanner flourished. By age twelve, his brain was astonishingly similar to those of other children of his age, and he was a straight-A student.

It's not just kids who benefit from brain plasticity but adults as well. A study of (pre-GPS) London cab drivers who were required to master navigating the city's convoluted geography found that they had an astonishing ability to choose the fastest route between two points. In fact, the navigational challenges these cab drivers faced stimulated brain development; that is, their brains were changed by the job, with larger-than-average memory centers.

Rather than sorting out the kids whose brains are already prepared to do math, we can and should design a learning system to build math brains. If we provide the right stimulation and experiences—the equivalent of asking cab drivers to navigate a maze of neighborhoods—they will rise to the challenge.

The Math Instinct

We aren't surprised when babies segue from coos and gurgles to speaking in full sentences. We prod the process by talking to them, even before they can understand us, and we know all the while that they *will* speak. Humans have a language instinct. I was surprised to learn that we also have a math instinct, an inborn number sense. And it's not just humans—primates, dolphins, and even birds (with their unfairly maligned brains) can count.

One of the hurdles to our understanding is the longtime influence of Jean Piaget, the child development expert who asserted that toddlers can't understand cause and effect or think logically. Piaget noted that toddlers are egocentric and cannot easily take the perspectives of others. He also believed that the ability to think logically came from trial and error only within the paradigm of formal education. Cutting-edge science has disproved his assertions. From the start, our brains are built for math, understanding quantities, cause and effect, and complex algebraic ideas of solving for *x*.

In fact, when a team of University of California, Berkeley, researchers compared solving for *x* between preschoolers and undergraduates, the preschoolers won. The contest also demonstrated that preschoolers innately understood the concept of multiple causality. The researchers presented preschoolers and undergraduates with the same machine, which they called a toy. The machine turned on, lighting up and making sounds when the right color or number of blocks were placed on the tray. There were two ways to succeed. The first was by placing a single blue block on the tray, and the second was by placing both an orange and a purple block on the tray. The researchers asked each group to use the blocks to turn on the toy. They asked them to play and experiment.

Each time they played the game, the young children did a better job than the undergrads. While both groups could determine that the blue block turned on the toy, through testing of cause and effect, the toddlers were more likely to discover they could also activate the machine by using two different-colored blocks. The researchers found that the undergraduates were burdened by a "single cause and single effect mentality" whereas the toddlers were more flexible and prepared to consider multiple causality.

If you still doubt the science on our natural math instinct, consider pigeons and primates. Pigeons not only can count but can learn abstract rules about numbers; their abilities were shown to be similar to those of primates. Primates can rank items on a screen from the lowest number of items to largest, even when the items differ in size and shape. They can even replicate the task when they are shown unfamiliar items. In other words, irrespective of the objects, primates have categorical knowledge that, for example, five is more than two.

Whether we're talking about birds and monkeys or undergrads and toddlers, the key finding is clear: math ability is not a rare gift. It is a basic instinct. If you've spent most of your life assuming that you or others are incapable of learning math, a few powerful datasets may help you to question that conclusion.

In 2012, I cofounded the nonprofit math learning platform Zearn. Because we're a nonprofit, resources on the Zearn platform are free. We are also able to focus on the long-term goal of math learning for all rather than the short-term goal of profit. Teachers loved our beta digital lessons, shared the site with their colleagues, and took it viral. In 2023, one in four elementary students and more than one million middle school students were active on the platform. Put another way, millions of students have completed billions of math problems on our site. As a result, we have one of the largest math learning datasets out there.

With our dataset, we can see when kids understand that $\frac{1}{4}$ is smaller than $\frac{1}{2}$, even though 4 is bigger than 2, and when they don't. With our software platform, we can then push code weekly to update the lessons so they better serve the needs of students. Our product managers and data scientists comb through the data to answer questions about the best ways to learn math. We consistently see something simple but profound: All students make learning gains, the more math they do. And we see the students who were previously lowest-scoring make the most gains. Why is that happening? Whatever was stopping them before, it wasn't that they were hitting the limits of their ability to learn. The conclusion we can draw from more than fourteen billion completed math problems is that we all have the math instinct and we can all grow our math brains.

We can also look at data outside of math to gain perspective. When I stumbled on this chart about literacy rates over time, I couldn't help but think about the assumptions folks were making in 1850 about the ability to read. Today we take it for granted that literacy can be taught, even though historically it was a rare skill. What were the systems and justifications that kept it so exceptional in the 1800s? What caused us to sort people rather than teach them? Finally—most interesting—why did we change?

Notice the slope of the line in this chart. Literacy gains increase gradually for one hundred years and then the slope becomes steep for another hundred years. While the slope is increasing, the human population on Earth is also exploding.

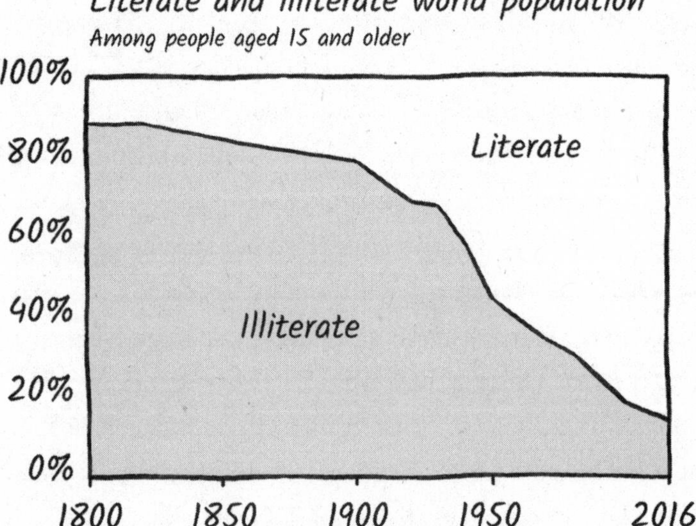

Source: Adapted from OurWorldinData.org/literacy (CC BY 4.0) (available at https://creativecommons.org/licenses/by/4.0/deed.en_US)

Another relevant set of data is US performance in math versus that of other OECD countries. In the 2022 international exam called the Program for International Student Assessment (PISA), US high school students ranked ninth in reading and sixteenth in science but thirty-fourth in math. In Europe and Asia, simply put, more children learn more math than in the United States. That is true any way you slice it. Just as significant, many of the countries now at the top were not anywhere near the top fifty years ago, namely every high-performing Asian country. If they can do it, we can, too. We can all be math people.

That's the epiphany I had over a lifetime of learning math as a student, applying math as a quantitative professional, and discovering how other people learn math. Though that epiphany was sufficiently powerful to cause me to walk away from a successful business career to start a nonprofit aimed at democratizing access to an excellent math education, I still hadn't pushed deep enough on my assumptions. Once I did, the world started to look different. The rest of this book covers what I learned on that journey and how you can apply it to a future we can all create, where math is for everyone.

Part I

THE MYTHS

"Ideology, n. An imaginary relationship to a real situation."

—KIM STANLEY ROBINSON, ***THE MINISTRY FOR THE FUTURE***

"Until you make the unconscious conscious,
it will direct your life and you will call it fate."

—CARL JUNG

THOUGH MANY PEOPLE SAY THEY HATE MATH, WHAT they really mean is they hated the things they did in math class. They hated the experience of nonstop time pressure, of memorizing meaningless formulas and procedures, and of being forced to solve problems the exact way the teacher said to do it.

They were miserable because their learning was built on myths—that speed is everything, that success depends solely upon memorizing procedures, that there's a single right way to do each problem, and that creativity should be shunned. Following these myths turns curious kids into math-phobic adults. It prevents us from being comfortable with math, from developing our skills and achieving great results in a wide variety of fields.

And it prevents us from loving math.

If you're like most people, you reacted to that last statement with skepticism. Love? A number of years ago, I tried to convince a group of influential policymakers that we could set the goal to help all kids learn and love math. When I said that, the room became quiet and many of the policymakers began fidgeting in their seats and exchanging glances. The silence became awkward. Finally, one person spoke, clearly embarrassed on my behalf and trying to spare me further perceived embarrassment: "Shalinee, let's get them to enjoy and learn math. They're not going to love it, come on."

But they can love it. Solving a math problem should feel good, like eating a chocolate chip cookie or hitting a home run. From a neuroscience perspective, we know this is true. Scientists have used magnetic resonance imaging scans that show the brain lighting up like the night sky on the Fourth of July when people solve problems or puzzles. These "Aha!" moments feel wonderful, and they should occur regularly as part of the math process. But they don't. Our math education system makes learning math a hellish experience—and we all come to believe it should be that way. These beliefs compound to an actual condition many experience: math anxiety.

- According to research conducted by the Miami-Dade County Public Schools, 93 percent of Americans feel some degree of math anxiety.

- In a survey of US teachers, 67 percent of them told the EdWeek Research Center that math anxiety was a challenge for their students, and 25 percent of the teachers reported they themselves experienced anxiety when doing math.

- The Organization for Economic Cooperation and Development (OECD) found that 30 percent of high school students reported feeling "helpless" when doing math problems.

- "People who are highly math anxious avoid math: They avoid elective coursework in math, both in high school and college, they avoid college majors that emphasize math, and they avoid career paths that involve math," shares Mark H. Ashcraft, a cognitive psychologist.

- A study revealed that some highly anxious math students sacrifice accuracy for speed, especially when they encounter difficult problems on tests. The theory is that these anxious students hurried to finish the test as fast as possible because doing it was such a stressful experience and they just wanted to be done with it.

Emerging cognitive and neuroscience research finds that math anxiety is not just a response to poor performance—in fact, four out of five students with math anxiety are average-to-high math performers. Rather, it is linked to higher activity in areas of the brain that relate to fear of failure *before* a math task, not *during* it. Of course we don't experience the pleasure of math. We have learned to dread math. *Math anxiety often overwhelms us even before we begin solving a problem.*

Does reading make people similarly anxious? Rarely, because there aren't the same myths attached to reading as there are to math. In psychology, there's a saying: Name it to tame it. If you can become aware of the condition that is causing you problems and identify it, you're in a much better position to manage its negative effects. While we have named "math anxiety," we haven't done the work to sufficiently unpack it, to understand it, and finally, to tame it. That is the aim of the next few chapters.

You're not wrong to feel resentment, fear, or boredom at what you encountered in math class. But what you encountered wasn't math.

CHAPTER 2

Speed Isn't Everything

THINK BACK TO ELEMENTARY SCHOOL MATH CLASS. IF you're like most Americans, you have a distinct memory of timed multiplication tests.

These weekly tests drilling you on 1 through 12 times 1 through 12 probably stressed you out. They turned math into a sprint to the finish line. Even if you did well, you may still feel your pulse quicken and your stomach knot when confronted with a page of multiplication problems.

Don't misunderstand me. For critical parts of math learning, speed matters. But speed isn't everything. The myth that speed is the defining feature of math success kills any chance of a love for math.

The Value of Speed

The truth is that kids don't have to be the fastest to be successful with math. We have an unfortunate history of swinging from underemphasizing to overemphasizing the value of speed; more on that later in the chapter. This overemphasis is especially nonsensical today, given the computing power of our digital devices. You may have heard someone assert that a smartphone possesses more power than the mainframe computer that helped astronauts land on the moon. This is an understatement. An iPhone 6, obsolete now, could guide 120 million Apollo-era spacecrafts to the moon simultaneously. Our run-of-the-mill devices are capable of computing at astonishing speeds.

In fact, we've become dependent on computing speed to provide basic services like electricity and telecommunications infrastructure. The PageRank algorithm, which brought us the Google search, is an exhibition of the transformative power of machines to do math quickly. The uncanny experiences you have when using generative AI, such as ChatGPT, at their core rely on mathematical models and breakthroughs in computing power. We no longer need humans to calculate quickly. We do, however, need people who slowly, methodically, and creatively consider how to use fast computing capabilities to solve hard and interesting problems.

Consider the evolution of how we build. Centuries ago, we relied on brute strength—human and animal. Engineering marvels such as the Great Pyramids of Egypt and the Great Wall of China were constructed without electric machine power. Not so long ago, if you were in charge of a building project, you'd hire the strongest people you could find and perhaps train work animals to assist you. Today, we rely on cranes, earth movers, and other heavy machinery to build skyscrapers, and there's no need to hire a champion bodybuilder to operate them. Instead, you hire people who are skilled at using cranes to their best advantage.

The emphasis on speed creates another significant problem; it can *decrease* rigor. Sian Beilock, the current president of Dartmouth College, studies human performance and specifically when humans underperform their potential. In her *New York Times* bestselling book, *Choke,* she shares the finding that more sophisticated math students solving more sophisticated math problems go more slowly than novices, to prevent panicking and choking under time pressure.

In one study, physics graduate students and professors, as well as undergraduates who had completed one physics class, were given physics problems to solve under time pressure. The problems were difficult but accessible to the undergraduates based on the course they had completed.

The scientists assumed that the graduate students and professors would finish with both greater speed and accuracy than the undergraduates, but they were surprised. The graduate students and professors did achieve much higher accuracy but took longer to complete the problems. Specifically, they took much longer to start and set up. Rather than succumbing to panic, the graduate students recognized how rushing could cause them to start the wrong way, ensuring that their labor would be wasted. Because they were experienced in solving complex math in the context of physics, they read and reread the prompts and slowed way down to consider where and how to start. They made up some time on the calculations, but they still came in second to the novices, the undergrads, who often misunderstood the problems in their rush, assuring their solutions were wrong. Knowing when to slow down is a problem-solving advantage.

When I listen to software engineers at Zearn grappling with a tough problem, I never hear or see anyone shouting out the first thing that comes into their head like third graders racing through their memorized multiplication tables. Instead, they spend time discussing the various aspects of the questions in front of them, framing complex problems in simpler pictures (for example, drawing the problem on a whiteboard). While they often run calculations using computers, their ability to analyze the problem, to bounce ideas off their fellow engineers, and to test possible options ultimately yields a solution. That the computer can run the numbers quickly is useful, but it's only one part of how the problem is solved.

When we overemphasize speed, we can implicitly or explicitly reduce problem-solving abilities. Jim Stigler, a legendary researcher in the field of how children learn mathematics, has studied differences in students' willingness to spend time struggling through problem-solving. In one study, he and researchers gave first graders an impossible math problem to work on. The American students worked for less than thirty seconds on average before giving up. Japanese first-graders, who generally perform better on mathematics exams than American first-graders, spent more than an hour struggling to solve the problems.

Freeing Up Working Memory

The Institute of Education Services (IES), part of the US Department of Education and a respected arbiter of what works in education, reviewed thousands of studies and concluded that to support students learning math and especially those struggling in math, "regular, timed activities to build up fluency" are critical. Don't those timed multiplication tests in third grade qualify as "timed activities"? Yes, they do.

If you dig a bit deeper into the institute's conclusion, you discover a valuable truth about speed and math. When you make part of the math solving process automatic, it saves brain power that can be directed at a given problem. In other words, when you don't have to think through every single calculation and you have efficient ways to calculate, or know many of the calculations automatically, then you can direct more of your brain energy toward learning new mathematics or solving the challenge in front of you. Repeated, timed activities are required to build fluency, and thus are an important part of math learning.

At the same time, when the timed activities are *all* a kid experiences, it sucks the creativity and pleasure (and even the rigor) out of doing math. Think of a piano student practicing only scales. Even from the beginning, piano students are given melodies, too, so they have something meaningful to which they apply the techniques they're learning. Otherwise, you might get really good at your scales, but you'd find the exercise and thus the piano itself dull and robotic. You would also likely show limited progress as a pianist.

Another way to understand the importance of speed or fluency in math is by drawing a parallel between brains and computers. When you buy a computer, you need to decide how much RAM (random access memory) to purchase—RAM determines the number of programs a computer can run simultaneously. A similarity exists between RAM and what we refer to as working memory in the human brain. In the 1890s, without modern scientific tools, American philosopher William James speculated about how the brain worked, and he got very close to what science has since found. He believed the brain worked through both primary memory, which lasts for a few seconds and holds information in our consciousness, and secondary memory, which has unlimited duration and can be brought to consciousness if desired. James's primary memory is what we now term working memory.

Since then, how memory works has been deeply studied by neuroscientists and psychologists. Secondary memory is commonly broken into two types—explicit and procedural. Separate parts of the brain are associated with distinct parts of memory. There is a famous story from the 1950s of a man named H.M. whose doctors removed a portion of his brain to try to reduce his suffering from seizures. What resulted was a strange form of amnesia. H.M. could carry on a conversation and perform tasks that required his working memory. But the next day, he wouldn't remember the conversation or recognize whom he'd met. His secondary memory had been harmed, but not all of it. If he had met you before the surgery, he still knew who you were. He couldn't store new explicit memories, such as names or facts, but hadn't lost his old ones. Further, both before and after the surgery, he could build new procedural memories: things like the fingering for piano pieces, knowledge of multiplication tables, or how to throw a football. Procedural memory is best defined as something you know how to do but you can't explain how you do it. It feels unconscious. Because you are fluent, it feels automatic. But he could not build new explicit memories, such as the names of people or places.

From pre-K through elementary school, our educational system works on developing children's working, explicit, and procedural memory. The youngest children's day starts with a structured routine—hang your things in your cubby, wash your hands, turn over your name rock so we know you're here, greet your teachers, and come sit in the morning circle—to go through each morning, until their working memory has mastered the once-difficult, multistep directions, and the tasks move to procedural memory.

Sometimes, of course, working memory doesn't work. You walk into your closet for something, but you can't remember what it is (this happens to me more often than I care to admit). Or your computer's working memory freezes, and both you and the computer have to figure out where you were once it restarts.

When students are trying to solve a math problem and they seem to know the discrete parts on homework assignments or tests, but they can't put it all together, it may be that their working memory is overloaded and it, too, freezes. To simplify a pre-algebraic equation, a seventh grader might need to multiply 6 × 7, and also subtract 17 – 9. These are ancillary tasks to the core of the problem, but she has to do them nonetheless. If getting to the answers, 42 and 8, takes too much of her working memory and all her RAM is being used, she may find herself standing in a metaphorical closet, befuddled. She can't remember where she is in the simplification of the equation.

If this student had increased her fluency of multiplication and subtraction facts by using timed activities as a learning strategy, those facts would be in her procedural memory. The recall of those facts would feel less effortful. That would allow her the space in her brain to solve the question. Her working memory would free up, and she could engage in the problem or participate in the new math learning.

This is why it is essential to develop fluency with certain math facts and processes. Speed counts for something. Just not for everything.

Integrative Complexity

Integrative complexity is a term that facilitates understanding of the "yes and no." It means that it's possible for two things to be true, even when they may seem in opposition (the definition of a paradox). Integrative complexity is also vital because it warns us to be wary of reductive truths—for example, math success is all about speed, or conversely, speed is irrelevant or harmful to math success. Many people refer to integrative complexity in the context of communicating the value of seeing shades of gray rather than black-and-white thinking. Throughout Part I as we navigate the myths, I will lean on integrative complexity to bring them to light.

Though I'm far from an expert about the launch and operations of the James Webb Space Telescope (JWST), I know enough to understand that this monumental feat helps us to see integrative complexity. One of my sons has put the telescope's first, startlingly beautiful images, the Cosmic Cliffs in the Carina Nebula, on his device as the background image. The telescope is a joint endeavor with NASA, the European Space Agency, and the Canadian Space Agency. It's a crowning achievement in mathematics and science that the entire human race can be proud of.

The JWST has four key goals: (1) to search for light from

the first stars and galaxies that formed in the universe after the Big Bang, (2) to study galaxy formation and evolution, (3) to understand star and planet formation, and (4) to study planetary systems and the origins of life.

Wait, how can the telescope find light from the first stars and galaxies after the Big Bang? The Big Bang was about 13.8 billion years ago, so this goal is achieved by looking into the distant past. Yep, time travel. Consider that it takes time for light to travel—for example, light leaving the sun takes a little over eight minutes to reach Earth. That means that when you enjoy a sunset, you are seeing the sun from eight minutes ago.

Similarly, the Webb telescope is observing light sent in the direction of Earth long ago, with the goal of seeing what the universe looked like about 250 million years after the Big Bang.

The hundreds of scientists, mathematicians, engineers, and technicians collaborating across numerous countries engineered this marvel by working methodically (mostly slowly), with high levels of fluency in mathematics (sometimes quickly). The first discussion of the JWST began in 1996 and then two concept studies began in 1999. Because the JWST was built on technology that didn't exist in 1999, it required innovation to dream up and then create, so two studies were commissioned. When the planning began, it was unknown if a telescope as large as Webb could be built with low enough mass to launch into space. Rather than let one team address this challenge, NASA asked two teams to explore it.

The telescope launched twenty-two years later in December 2021, ten years after the construction and fabrication was complete. The planning had begun twelve years earlier than that. Further, unlike the Hubble telescope, the Webb was going to orbit the sun at a distance from Earth too far to be repaired. There was a lot of math at stake.

Despite stories like this one, we still often believe that, in math, speed is the defining feature of math success. We confuse ourselves into believing that initial speed determines who even should learn mathematics. We also rarely bother to tell students the vital purpose of speed is to build fluency, not to compete to be the fastest at easy calculations. Perhaps we've all seen too many movies featuring math geniuses solving complex problems at lightning speed. The myth persists. Where did it come from?

Math education isn't often discussed from an integrative complexity perspective, with requisite speed and fluency counterbalanced by a slower, more creative and collaborative approach. Both-and, not either-or. The problem can be traced back to the math wars, a phrase coined in the 1990s but a battle that has been fought in schools for at least fifty years. At the time of this writing, I am nervous that the math wars may be revving up again. This should worry us all. The only casualties are the students.

The math wars are more like World War I than World War II. In World War II, the narrative is about the good guys and the bad guys, the Allies (i.e., democracies) and the Axis (i.e., Nazis). Trying to parse WWI, meanwhile, is much trickier. The common explanation is that a series of treaties created a domino effect engulfing multiple continents in war. The dominos began falling due to the assassination of an archduke. In the end, forty million people died. Similarly, the math wars are complex without easily identifiable good guys and bad guys. In fact, it is often not clear to many educators or STEM workers, like my team of software engineers and technologists, what the math wars are about; the issues ebb and flow with the political tides. Further, the math wars morph as social media celebrities seek Likes, and factions come together and dissolve. As it pertains to speed and math, the wars are quite simple: One side overemphasizes it and the other side underemphasizes it.

The research doesn't declare a clear winner in the battle over speed. The problem is that neither side is willing to acknowledge the integrative complexity that the research offers and strike the proper balance. Rather than take a pragmatic approach, the two camps are debating their pure ideologies while students lose out. They are certainly not interested in observing the practical usefulness of their ideas. In 2008, the National Mathematics Advisory Panel called out the warring camps in their final report, stating: "To prepare students for Algebra, the curriculum must simultaneously develop conceptual understanding, computational fluency, and problem-solving skills. Debates regarding the relative importance of these aspects of mathematical knowledge are misguided. These capabilities are mutually supportive, each facilitating learning of the others." It is evident that neither camp listened to the National Mathematics Advisory Panel.

In other affluent countries, math students regularly outperform students in the US, and this is in part due to their ability to strike a balance between the two camps. The goal of math teaching and learning in those countries is to develop enough fluency of math facts to free up working memory so students can solve interesting problems, while also teaching them to slow down, like the expert physics graduate students, to tackle complex problems.

As is the case with most wars, this one has historical roots. While it is rarely mentioned, it is vital to remember before getting too enthusiastic about taking a side that they begin with whether or not to teach math at all. In the early 1900s, William Heard Kilpatrick, a protégé of John Dewey and one of the originators of modern math pedagogy, deemed math an "intellectual luxury" and "harmful rather than helpful to the kind of thinking necessary for ordinary living." Kilpatrick's contemporary, David Snedden, a Columbia Teachers College professor and later the Massachusetts education commissioner, called algebra a "nonfunctional and nearly valueless subject for 90 percent of boys and 99 percent of girls." Whether adversaries in the math wars know it or not, some of their positions originally were developed by those who lived in another century and world and were simply against teaching advanced math at all except to the elite.

University of California, Berkeley, professor Alan H. Schoenfeld has documented more than a century's worth of seesaw opinions on math and the resulting changes in what was taught and how. For example, the share of students enrolled in algebra fell dramatically from 57 percent in 1909 to less than 25 percent by 1955, as the early anti-math coalition influenced policy, teaching, and learning.

During World War II, this initial pro-math versus anti-math alignment broke apart. Political leaders took notice that army recruits needed to be trained in bookkeeping and gunnery, which require foundational math abilities. Afterward, a full math panic occurred during the Cold War in the 1950s, focusing on conceptual math learning and pushing for advanced math once again. During this time, algebra returned to high schools and calculus found its way into high school for the first time. Since then, every twenty to thirty years, in the 1970s, 1990s, and perhaps in the 2020s, the math wars have kicked off. (But let's hope not again.)

While neither camp still believes that math has no value to "99 percent of girls," the positions taken are often as odd and difficult to grapple with for people in the real world, especially the real world of STEM. For example, a common fight in the math wars that has manifested each time is the debate to pit "procedural fluency" against "conceptual understanding" or vice versa. To decode that jargon for you, "procedural fluency" means knowing how to do the multiplication algorithm if you are asked what 43 × 9 equals. In layman's terms, the multiplication algorithm is when you stack the numbers and "carry" to get to the product.

Conceptual understanding is about knowing what is even being asked of you. If I ask you if the product of 43 × 9 is bigger or smaller than 430—and how you figured that out—you might say, "It would be smaller because 43 × 10 = 430 so it would be exactly one unit of 43 smaller, or 387."

This would be as if English teachers debated whether it was paramount to be able to read the words *procedure* and *concept* or more important to know what the words meant. Or if doctors debated whether it was vital that your heart or brain was getting oxygen and blood. Both are critical. Pitting these two crucial parts of reading, math, or being alive against each other is nonsensical. Math teachers, parents, people starting small businesses, and a classroom of kindergartners know that you need to know both how to do math and what the math you are doing means.

The myth of speed that has shaped nearly all our math identities, usually negatively, comes from this mess. Either we never spent enough time with timed activities to support our ability to learn advanced math or we engaged in so many timed tests that we came to dislike math altogether. It's hard to hear but key to know that the math wars are not even nefarious. They are mostly confused ideology that has shaped the last century of education.

Several years ago, I was invited to visit a group of elementary schools in Northern California by a math coach named Sheila. We spent the day walking through dozens of classrooms, watching elementary math in action. I was in awe of the teachers and the math coach's effort and dedication.

As the school day wrapped up, we grabbed a table in the teachers' lounge. Sheila opened her computer, pulled up a spreadsheet, and sat there without speaking. I tried to process what was on her screen. It looked like a set of tables and charts that showed the number of seconds it took for hundreds of children to answer all their multiplication facts. I had no idea what I was supposed to do with this information.

I said, "Thank you for sharing this impressive collection of data. How can I be helpful?"

Sheila told me about the effort and care that had gone into getting the data. She described all the work they had done to help children memorize their math facts—using songs, flashcards, and contests with prizes. But despite all this labor, Sheila wasn't satisfied with the result. The data showed many children who could accurately say that 6 × 6 = 36, or that 9 × 9 = 81, within three or four seconds of being asked. What else could they do, she asked me, to help those kids deliver their answers in two seconds?

I paused. "Why is this important?" I asked.

Sheila didn't understand my question. Trying to clarify what I meant, I was more specific: "Why is it relevant for a student to move from taking three or four seconds to answer 9 × 9 to two seconds?"

She looked at me as if I had asked why she thought the world was round. "That's the definition," she said. "They need to have automaticity of their math facts for future math success. Automaticity means recall in two seconds or less. That's the definition!"

I asked her if there was research she could pass along, showing how researchers had settled on two seconds rather than three seconds or even five seconds as the threshold for automatic recall. She didn't have any. I have since searched for any causal study showing that knowing your math facts in three seconds versus two seconds matters for real life. I have not found one.

Sheila was a dedicated and talented educator who had found a way to scale herself to serve dozens of classrooms and hundreds of students. Her sincerity had been coopted, however, by a faulty premise—the myth that speed was everything. She deeply believed that automaticity of all the multiplication facts was a key to future success, and that automaticity meant spitting out the facts in two seconds or less. She had taken the myth of speed too far.

Perhaps you had the experience as I did in early math education of nonstop timed tests and thus failing to finish a math test in the allotted time. The teacher called, "Time's up," and you still had problems unanswered. You endured that stomach-dropping feeling of having work left to do when the teacher said pencils down. And you received a poor grade or score because you couldn't finish on time.

As a result of this "failure," you may have learned some of these lessons:

- If I can't solve a problem in under one minute (or whatever short time frame), it isn't worth the effort. There are other people who can solve this problem in one minute, so this problem is for them, not me.

- I must be stupid in math and shouldn't pursue this area of study because I'm so slow.

- It's impossible to build your mathematical and reasoning brain in the same way you build your ability in other subjects or how you build your physical ability in sports; there's no point in working at math if you're slow.

- Memorizing arbitrary rules and facts, not reasoning or critical thinking, is what defines success.

All these false conclusions contribute to math anxiety and math aversion. They cause us to stop trying and it becomes a self-fulfilling prophecy—the more we believe we're bad at math, the more we avoid it and the worse we get at it.

I recognize the situational value of timed tests and speed. We utilize timed strategies in Zearn, as our testing and learning show it is important for students. Beyond the need to build fluency, there is only so much time allotted to classes daily, and if there weren't timed tests and strict deadlines, students might never finish anything. I also understand that the ability to work fast allows people to get things done when they need to get done—the fast typist has an advantage over the slow one, businesses and newspapers have tight deadlines, scientists have to race against the clock to develop vaccines.

But when speed is the *primary* goal, many kids are turned off and never develop skills that can be crucial in whatever careers they eventually pursue.

We need to keep in mind the realities that counteract the myth of speed:

- Math is one of the few areas of life with no arbitrary rules and relatively few things to memorize. In many ways, it is an open system that rewards contemplation and exploration.

- Contrary to common belief, math is a team sport. Solutions to difficult problems emerge through slower collaboration, not through an individual trying to finish her work as fast as possible.

- Math at its core is really just reasoning or critical thinking. This takes time, especially when we're tackling a big problem. It requires us to find courage and calmness, to break the problem into smaller pieces, solve each smaller problem, and then put it all back together for the big solution.

- Math can be hard, and hard things can take time. But hard doesn't mean impossible or onerous or anxiety-producing. Like a lot of things worth doing, math requires hard work.

Research shows that one mindset that supports learning math, rock climbing, or acquiring any worthwhile competency centers on coming to accept and enjoy doing hard things. The myth of speed creates an alternative reality, one in which we think because we don't have an innate and mythic speed, we should avoid math altogether (or try to get through it with as little effort as possible). We don't instead consider that we should build up speed even though it can be hard. It's hard to read Shakespeare. It's hard to learn yoga. It's hard to play a musical instrument. But just about anyone can learn to do these hard things and gain tremendous enjoyment and benefit from doing them.

Keeping this in mind helps avoid a fixed mindset—a mindset that causes math to be seen as impossibly difficult, boring, and anxiety-producing. Research about student perception of the ability to do a given academic task reveals two orientations. The first is an *incremental* orientation, one in which students believe their ability is malleable, improving with effort. The second is an *entity* orientation, suggesting that ability is fixed and doesn't improve with effort.

The latter, of course, causes students who aren't as fast as their peers to believe that they're bad at math and this will never change. The former recognizes that even if they struggle with finishing the test or if they can't figure out problems, they will become better with practice. This much more optimistic and realistic orientation is what we will explore in Part II. This orientation helps kids succeed, no matter how much time it takes them to figure out a problem.

CHAPTER 3

Tricks Are Not the Answer

MEMORIZING TRICKS IS USEFUL FOR MAGICIANS OR con artists, not so much for people who want to learn and love math. For many students, math instruction seems about just that. For example, $3 \times 0 = 0$; $8 \times 0 = 0$; and $N \times 0 = 0$. Have you ever wondered *why* something times zero equals zero? Don't worry about it; memorize it. (More on the actual why later).

While tricks might get you good grades, you won't be good at math in the larger sense of the word. You won't particularly enjoy doing math, and you won't be able to translate your math sense into real-world problem-solving. In the world of teaching and learning or brain science, we call this transfer, being able to apply your learning in a new context. Relying on memorization and tricks robs you of abilities that are crucial to making the most of math.

As with the myth of speed, when we consider the myth of tricks, integrative complexity again is relevant. In contrast to rote memorization, the algorithms and procedures are essential and useful—as long as you understand them. These are tools that help us do math, but they're not the be-all and end-all of math.

Take algorithms. First, what is an algorithm? Before we get to the kind of artificial intelligence that conjures images from your imagination or writes a proficient five-paragraph essay, let's start with the basics. An algorithm is a sequence of rules or instructions that help us solve a specific problem or computation. The precise steps to make an almond butter and banana sandwich is an algorithm. The litmus test for an algorithm is that if you follow these steps, you always get an almond butter and banana sandwich.

The addition algorithm often taught around second grade is just this, and it is something you still likely use all the time. Perhaps you scribbled it in the corner of a page today. Let's say you are adding 128 to 437. Your first step might be to stack the numbers on top of each other, draw

a line underneath, and begin adding, right to left, and carrying the "1" to the next place value position. Those steps to add numbers are an algorithm, often referred to as the standard addition algorithm.

Algorithms, unlike tricks, are fabulous because they always work. They provide us something to build on. We can't solve harder problems without them. We should use algorithms, but we should also view them as tools and starting points, developing new and better methods, even better algorithms, from them. That is what is happening in the world of machine-learning algorithms and generative AI, which is astounding, amusing, and sometimes terrifying. In math, if you don't understand the algorithm, you limit your learning progress. For example, without actually understanding why the addition algorithm works, when students turn to use the subtraction algorithm, they often struggle: 308 – 271 = ?.

A good way to understand the limits of memorizing tricks is by recognizing what it can't help us do.

You Can't Memorize How to Be Intuitive

The damage that math myths do often occurs subtly rather than overtly. The obvious fallout—memorization and formulas turn math into a dull, robotic process—is bad enough. But here are three destructive effects that often occur beyond our awareness.

Diminished Common Sense

I know that 10 classrooms of 20 kids will have more kids than 6 classrooms of 20 kids. I don't have to follow a mathematical formula to know this.

$$(10)(20) - (6)(20) =$$

I don't need to calculate at all!

Instead, I can rely on common sense—or intuition, if you prefer—to come to this conclusion. Forget the number of kids per classroom, since all classrooms have equal numbers of students. Ten classrooms are more than six. When we filter our reasoning through memorized rules or procedures, we fail to take advantage of our innate ability to figure things out.

Numeracy is innate, and we should feel confident that we have it in the same way we possess the ability to learn language. As mentioned in Chapter 1, scientists have proven that babies and toddlers show and develop numeracy early on; babies only a few days old can distinguish two from three. Birds and of course chimpanzees and other primates have innate numeracy as well. At the same time, this natural instinct can't be taken for granted. Use it or lose it—we need to use our number sense regularly or this mental muscle will atrophy.

Less Creativity, Curiosity, and Play

Creativity requires a willingness to experiment, to be sufficiently brave and try something new or different. People who risk doing something creative may fail, but they try anyway. Relying on memorized directions prevents kids from taking chances, from finding their own way to solve a problem. They come to believe that there's one way, and one way only, to solve it. Curiosity requires questions and an open space to explore. The creative spark or insatiable curiosity that are at the heart of many mathematical breakthroughs is extinguished. Creativity and curiosity also often exist in a space of play. Play is open-ended and exploratory. You don't play by going through memorized steps that you don't understand. But problem-solving can be play, and I would offer to you that only when it is play do we arrive at breakthroughs.

Less Perspective

Consider this math problem and how it can be solved:

$$1000 + 700 + 80 - 90 + 6 - 700 + 90 - 4 =$$

$$1000 + 700 + 80 = 1780 \qquad -700 - 90 + 6 = -784 \qquad 90 - 4 = 86$$

$$1780 + 86 = 1866$$

$$1866 - 784 = 1082$$

Here are the steps I might take to solve this problem if I just jump in without stepping back. I needed to do about five calculations, and I also checked my work, making it ten calculations. Because the calculations depend upon each other, I got nervous as I moved through this problem, hoping I wasn't carrying an initial mistake all the way through to the end.

There's a better way to address this problem if you are able to retain perspective and a bit of common sense:

$$1000 + 700 + 80 - 90 + 6 - 700 + 90 - 4 =$$
$$1000 + \cancel{700} + 80 - \cancel{90} + 6 - \cancel{700} + \cancel{90} - 4 =$$
$$1000 + 80 + 6 - 4 =$$
$$1082$$

As you can see, taking a step back to gain perspective on the whole problem is key. Rather than solving by adhering rigidly to the order of the numbers, we can take it in as a whole and reduce the steps needed to solve it from five-ten to one-two. Further, from that new vantage point, I am also much more certain that I am right.

Several years back, a high school math teacher, Ben Orlin, wrote an *Atlantic* article titled "When Memorization Gets in the Way of Learning," and it quickly became a favorite of mine, since Orlin captures the problem with memorization humorously and thought-provokingly. He begins by describing teaching his first high school trigonometry class and asking the students, "What is the sine of $\frac{\pi}{2}$?"

The class all responded with the answer, 1, which they said they learned the previous year.

Let me quote from Orlin's article, since it so perfectly captures the problem here: ". . . they really didn't know what sine even meant. They'd simply memorized the fact. To them, math wasn't a process of logical discovery and thoughtful exploration. It was a call-and-response game. Trigonometry was just a collection of non-rhyming lyrics to the lamest sing-along ever." Just memorizing facts or rules in any subject prevents real understanding and enjoyment. We need to grasp the larger context, the way a formula connects to other concepts.

The other problem with memorizing is that we forget. Do you recall the date of the Battle of Hastings, the location of Belgium on a map, the eleventh president of the United States? To pass a test, you had to memorize these or similar facts. Once the test was over or shortly thereafter, your mind wiped them from your consciousness. When we understand what we've memorized, we are much more likely to remember.

This is referred to as chunking or congruent memory making. For example, it is easier to remember a list of items that are related (many colors) than one that is unrelated (items on my coffee table). Our brain automatically uses chunks and patterns as a scaffold. In fact, neuroscientists have demonstrated through brain scans that the brain works differently when engaging in congruent memory making (purple, yellow, green, teal) than incongruent memory making (graphic novel, calculator, charger, Lego piece, magazine, coin).

And not only does the brain work differently, it works better. Humans are better at congruent memory making than incongruent memory making. When the new thing we learned connects to something we already understand, or if we can group the learning into a chunk of understanding rather than a random list, we can retain and apply the new learning far more readily.

The Times Zero Rule

Understanding opens the mind to possibilities; it provides insights about the way things work; it serves as a catalyst for more learning.

Why is anything multiplied by zero, zero? I love to ask this question of people who do high-level math professionally—professors, tech leaders, engineers, and so on—and they usually have to stop and think. They say, "Well, it's called a convention. In math, we have those." Like most of us, they've accepted the rule without understanding it.

I was guilty of this unquestioning acceptance, even after college, graduate school, and working in an analytic role cutting big datasets. Eventually, though, I was taught the reason, and it blew me away. I love that I understand why, and I am so excited to share it with you.

Think of multiplication as plates of cookies. 3 × 1 means I have 3 plates, and each plate has 1 cookie. So that is 3 cookies altogether. And 3 × 3 means I still have 3 plates, but each plate now has 3 cookies. That is 9 cookies altogether. Here are illustrations of some warm, gooey, fresh chocolate chip cookies. (At times, I have baked cookies with my twin sons to illustrate this point. That's the only reason we bake cookies, really—to help everyone learn and love math.)

This is the meaning of multiplication made concrete. That's what the symbol is saying: The first number is the number of groups (plates) and the second number is the number of items (cookies). Now express 3 × 0 in plates and cookies. Okay, that is 3 plates. And how many cookies are on each plate? Zero. So now instead of 3 plates with 3 or 9 warm, gooey cookies, I have zero cookies in total. No cookies!

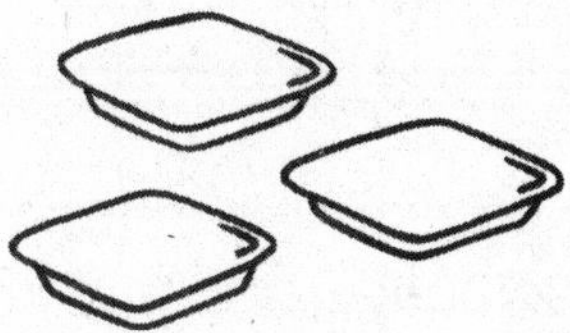

With this understanding, you no longer have to rely on a memorized rule. Instead, you can summon the image of plates without cookies and grasp why anything times zero is always zero. This visual aid means you can reduce the stress and time-suck that rule reliance causes. Even more important is that understanding the why creates trust. If you know why a given rule is true, then eventually you will grasp that there is always a why in math. When you trust math to make sense, you're free to explore, play, and find the boundaries of the rules. Once you know why the rules are true at their axiomatic level, you can see the beauty of math.

Similarly, consider the addition and subtraction of negative numbers:

$$-5 + -5 = ?$$
$$-5 + 5 = ?$$

Do you remember being taught negative numbers with an arbitrary list of rules? While nearly everyone I encounter learned the times zero rule as one to simply memorize, not everyone got the arbitrary list of rules for positive and negative numbers operations. Count yourself lucky if this wasn't drilled into your head. Most people I talk to were forced to learn and adhere to these rules without understanding them.

Integer Sign	Operation	Answer Sign
⊕ + ⊕	Add	⊕
⊖ + ⊖	Add	⊖
⊕ + ⊖	Subtract	Larger Integer's Sign
⊖ + ⊕	Subtract	Larger Integer's Sign

When you see two minus signs, it becomes a plus sign. I remember that I felt horror when I was taught these rules. All of a sudden, addition, which I had considered my friend, even a power, required a chart!? I distinctly remember thinking, "If two minus signs become a plus sign, then why not use a plus sign to begin with? Are these people crazy?" I also thought I would be defeated by negative numbers unless I could tattoo the chart onto my body.

I had the sense that these rules would be crucial for future math, but I was unsure of how I would remember them. Did they have a logic I could hold on to? Or were they just an arbitrary set of rules?

One day when I was eleven, my father walked by as I was doing my math homework, and he noticed my frustration. I was muttering to myself and maybe even snapping pencils in half. He saw that I was going through the motions without understanding what I was doing. I had a printed chart like this on the rules of negative numbers and I was trying to follow it like it was a secret decoder ring from a cereal box. He sat next to me and drew this picture in my notebook:

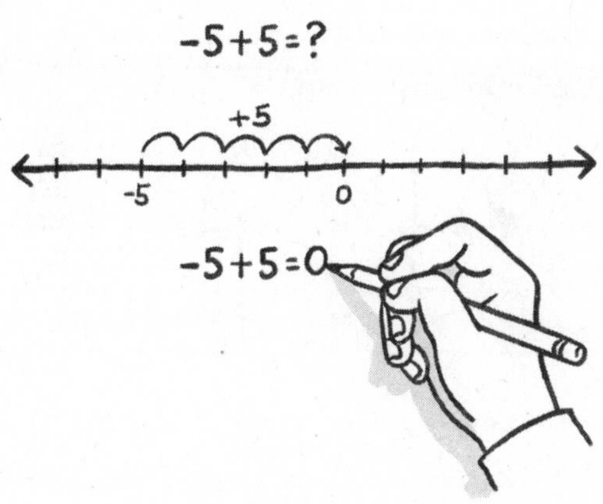

The positive and negative values, my dad said, were not arbitrary signs but rather the location of the number on the number line. If you were at the position -5 on the number line, adding 5 meant that you needed to move five spots in a positive direction. That would put you at 0. He said that if I understood that, I would never think of the confusing rules again: "Just remember the number line."

I released the rules that I could barely grasp from my brain, and I understood. Adding -5 to -5 would move you five more spots in the negative direction, to -10. I was on the path to building my math mind. My worries about turning in my homework the next day disappeared. It was one of the first moments when I realized another way existed to process the numbers in front of me and that when I was confused, I could push to deep understanding rather than trying harder to memorize.

The Trouble with Tricks

Were you ever taught the "bow tie" method to multiply two-digit numbers or to add fractions? Do you remember it now? Do you know why it worked?

Let's examine the bow tie method trick to add fractions.

Bow Tie Method

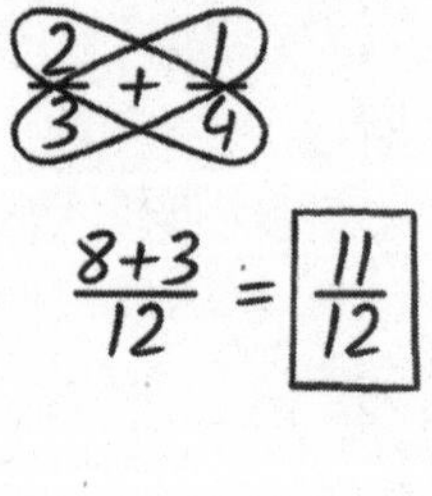

$$\frac{2}{3} + \frac{1}{4}$$

$$\frac{8+3}{12} = \boxed{\frac{11}{12}}$$

In this method, you first draw an oval to cover the 2 and the 4, and you multiply them together to get 8, and you write that number below. You do the same thing and draw the next oval and get 3. Write that below. (That's your bow tie.) You then multiply the two bottom numbers to get 12, and write the 12 below. Add 8 and 3. Voilà, the answer $\frac{11}{12}$. Great. But why does this work? And what happens if you forget the steps? Did you learn anything you could use to reason it through? Or did you learn an idea that helps you get started when you are stuck? And then what happens when you add three fractions instead of two?

$$\frac{2}{3} + \frac{1}{4} + \frac{1}{5} = ?$$

Where do you draw the bows now? Does the bow tie turn into a tangled mess?

This is a neat trick, but if you just learn the trick, you miss out on the first principles that explain why it works. For example, do you know that $\frac{8}{12}$ and $\frac{2}{3}$ have the exact same value? If you go to school for eight out of twelve months of the year, is that the same as going to school for $\frac{2}{3}$ of the year? Knowing this fact deepens the experience, removing it from numbers on a page and translating it into a tangible life experience. It's memorable, and it's useful.

Perhaps you were taught to follow the flip-and-multiply rule for dividing fractions. What does dividing by a fraction even mean? When would you ever even divide something by a fraction? What is 2 divided by $\frac{1}{2}$?

Here's the flip-and-multiply rule.

$$2 \div \frac{1}{2} =$$
$$\downarrow$$
$$2 \times \frac{2}{1} =$$
$$\downarrow$$
$$2 \times 2 = 4$$

This flip technique is far less worrisome than the bow tie method. And if a third divisor were to appear and the equation got longer, it would still work, since you can keep flipping and multiplying. This is an algorithm on solid footing rather than a trick like the bow tie, something that works only in certain conditions.

Again, however, this algorithm needs to be paired with understanding. When you add whole numbers like 38 + 75 using the addition algorithm, the traditional way you learned to stack numbers, you know the sum will be bigger at the end. That is because you get it—you grasp the logic of how two numbers added together yield a larger number.

Now ask yourself: When you divide 2 by $\frac{1}{2}$, will the resulting number be bigger or smaller at the end? Why? Do you have strong intuition? Can you tell a story that explains your answer? For 38 + 75, you can provide such a story: You have 38 students in kindergarten and 75 in first and second grade. How many students are there in K–2? You can create a variety of stories, all of which illustrate the principle.

Can you think of a story from your past where you have divided something by a fraction? For example, what if you had 2 cookies and you cut them up into halves (divided by $\frac{1}{2}$). How many pieces of cookies would you have? What real-life situation might cause you to cut them up in this manner? Perhaps you have four friends over, but you have only 2 cookies and everyone wants to try one. If you divide 2 by $\frac{1}{2}$, will you have enough? Yes.

This example helps reveal the actual meaning of the algorithm. Just as you know that when you add two positive numbers, the sum will be bigger, when you divide a number by a fraction, you will obtain a bigger number. You had 2 cookies, you divided them in half, and now you have 4 pieces of cookie to share.

The most frightening part of math tricks is that they don't always work. Math is what we rely on to always work: 2 + 2 is always 4. And if the engineers calculate correctly, the bridge will not fall down while you drive over it.

For instance, here's a guideline that doesn't always work that you might have been taught: When you multiply, the numbers get bigger, and when you divide, the numbers get smaller. This is often presented as an axiom, but it is a rickety crutch. The problem: This guideline works only in third grade, where you experience multiplication and division with positive whole numbers only. By fourth and fifth grades, when you are multiplying with decimals, the numbers sometimes get smaller and sometimes get bigger. In middle school, too, you are taught negative numbers, and the trick doesn't work with them either.

Tricks, by definition, can be deceptive—they may seem to work, we start to rely on them, and then they fail us. As Dr. Hilary Kreisberg, director of the Center for Mathematics Achievement at Lesley University, says:

> *It boggles my mind that some might associate the word "trick" with "learning," especially after seeing the various definitions. One interpretation of a trick is an illusion (or a false idea). Another definition is "liable to fail." This is exactly why we need to stop teaching children tricks in mathematics. The tricks are liable to fail once they've "expired," and they create false perceptions that they always work.*

On the other hand, mathematical principles and axioms exist that are as reliable as the sun rising every morning—and yet we hide them. Perhaps we think the why is too hard for kids to understand or for teachers to teach. Maybe it seems like a luxury or a waste of time. Whatever the reason, we must start teaching axioms, not sleight of hand.

Keep in mind that I'm a believer in integrative complexity—blending an algorithm with the "why" is what provides real value. Recognize, too, that not all tricks are the same. The tricks we can rely on are algorithms, which don't expire. Math presented with tricks you can't count on is in fact not math at all. They destroy positive math identities, sometimes forever. Reflecting on the specific examples I shared, I want to underline that this is serious stuff. Relying on tricks is a formula for failing to understand math, at worst, and for not particularly enjoying it, at best.

The Algorithm and the Blender

Between the blur of middle school math and the advent of machine learning, it might seem that algorithms that were once merely confusing are now impossible to understand. While we may not understand how to construct every algorithm, that doesn't absolve us from applying ourselves to learn how to use and how *not* to use them. Algorithms are like your kitchen blender, handy devices for frequent use. Algorithms are also our common history.

The word comes from a single man who lived in the eighth century CE in the kingdom of Khwarezm, in modern-day Turkmenistan and Uzbekistan. The word *algorithm* is the Latinization of his last name; his full name was Muhammad ibn Musa al-Khwarizmi. He was an astronomer, geographer, and mathematician, and he wrote a book titled *Al-Khwarizmi on the Hindu Art of Reckoning,* also referred to as *On Calculation with Hindu Numerals.* In those pages, Al-Khwarizmi laid out the system he found in texts created by another legendary mathematician, the astronomer Brahmagupta, who lived in India in the seventh century CE.

The texts showed a remarkable and practical system to represent any number on earth with just the following symbols: 1, 2, 3, 4, 5, 6, 7, 8, 9, 0, and . (a decimal point). Before this system, people represented numbers in a variety of ways, none as easy to use for calculations. The most familiar to us would be the Roman numeral system still in use for special occasions, such as denoting book chapters, gracing building edifices, or keeping track of the Super Bowl.

Since the twelfth century, the system to represent any number on earth with those symbols is universal. There is no Tower of Babel in math; we all can understand one another. It's an ingenious structure that always works. It's not a trick. In all other domains, we are separated by disparate languages with distinct written systems. In math, we can all write down the number 4 the same way in every part of the earth to ask for four glasses of water. And this convention has held across billions of people for almost a millennium.

Al-Khwarizmi loved the pure mathematics this structure allowed, but he also saw its practical application for everyone from merchants to shopkeepers. His book took off (we would call it going viral) and before long, the entire span of the Islamic world switched to this system. Though we think of them simply as numbers, historians call them Hindu-Arabic numerals. When his book was translated to Latin in the twelfth century, Europe also switched over.

And thus Al-Khwarizmi became famous; he became the algorithm.

As I said, I like to think of algorithms like a trusty blender. I don't know how to build one. If you were to provide me with the dozens of parts necessary for its construction, I could not assemble them into a working machine. But I know enough to operate the blender. I'm aware of which setting crushes ice. Even when I have a blender with which I'm unfamiliar, if I want to crush ice, I know enough to keep turning the power setting higher until we get there. I figured that out through experimentation and play. I was not afraid of the blender. I do not feel disempowered by the blender. I did not memorize the blender manual.

When I'm confronted by math or technology I don't understand, I find this analogy useful. If I add 38 + 75 and get 43, I immediately know I am wrong; 43 is a smaller number than one of my addends, 75. I have added only the 5, and in my haste, I have forgotten to add the 70. As we move through math, we need to obtain sufficient understanding of the why to estimate our answer and have a gut feel for when we are totally wrong.

To destroy the myth of math as memorizing tricks, we must dive into algorithms, especially how to use and not use them. We must separate unreliable tricks from steady algorithms. Again, keep the principle of integrative complexity in mind when considering this myth. Yes, mathematicians rely on algorithms, memorization, and other shortcuts, but they also develop and deepen their mathematical thinking.

Mathematical thinking is about examining a problem and reasoning it out, using a few rules or axioms. It should be fun, like solving a puzzle. And it involves a constant intuition about the math involved. Without that understanding and intuition, we're just going through the computational motions, deriving as much satisfaction and enjoyment from the process as our computers but likely with less accuracy than our computers, because we don't understand or even detect our mistakes.

CHAPTER 4

There Is No Single Way

TEACHING MATH AS IF THERE'S ONLY ONE CORRECT way to solve a problem makes us think that we're problem-solving, but instead, we're "answer-getting." I've seen it so many times, but none bothers me more than watching elementary and middle school students solve word problems in this way. Consider this typical middle school prompt: *A store is selling 6 bags of marbles for $18. What is the unit price for a bag of marbles?*

When I read this problem, I picture a child looking up at me and asking, "Does 'of' mean multiplication?" It has happened to me so many times when I visit math classrooms.

There's no secret code. *Of* could mean "multiply," but it might not. These are the highly counterproductive questions that children ask when they have been presented with a "single way" to solve word problems, such as looking for keywords. In this example, the students will immediately multiply 6 × 18. If you ask them why the unit price of a single bag of marbles would cost $108, and be so much more than the price of 6 bags of marbles, they will look at you with uncertainty. This is the process of answer-getting.

Problem-solving is a distinct cognitive experience. Instead, we ask, what is happening in the problem? It is not mindlessly following a single prescriptive set of steps. The way to solve this problem and every problem is to understand what is happening in the problem. But that means there will be many paths to the answer. How I understand the problem might be quite unlike how you understand it.

My advice is to first make a movie in your mind. This is my movie. I imagine a store and conjure a bin full of marble bags in front of me. There is a sign above the bin that reads "6 BAGS FOR $18." Looking at the bins, I only have the money and, frankly, the interest in one bag of marbles. What am I going to ask the checkout clerk? I divide $18 by 6 and ask if I can buy one bag of marbles for $3. So in this story problem, *of* has nothing to do with mathematics. It's a preposition clarifying what is inside the bags: marbles.

The latter is what math is really about, but math learning can feel like an ever-tightening vice. Who is still making movies in their minds when we are told that math is a series of precisely established steps that we must meticulously copy? What does understanding have to do with plugging and chugging?

In this answer-getting environment, we follow the prescribed steps and get the answer, but we often don't understand the steps. Most of all, we have no intuition as to whether we are in the ballpark. The implicit belief that we don't need our intuition is toxic. We end up engaging in math mimicry—doing exactly what we're told, a boring and mindless exercise.

But math isn't boring and mindless, or at least it shouldn't be. Problem-solving is challenging, engaging, creative, and ultimately, satisfying. Few of us, unfortunately, experience math in this manner because when we learn math, we come to believe the myth that there is a single right way to solve each problem.

The Right Way Is the Wrong Way

When we are taught to rely on a singular, step-by-step process as the true way to solve a math problem, we turn off our problem-solving brain. Over the years, we may lose at least some of our problem-solving acumen by not using it. These skills require continuous work to keep them sharp, and the constant reliance on someone else's "exact right" method dulls them. This reliance also discourages courage—we need to take chances to solve problems, and insistence on following a singular method prevents us from risking wrong answers via experimentation.

We can solve problems in many distinct ways. In fact, trying different approaches is fun as well as instructive, and it is necessary when problem-solving gets hard—which is often when the problems are most worth solving. Engineers who write software code or build bridges make a conscious attempt to solve problems in more than one way, even when a solution is readily available to them. Why not solve it and move on?

First of all, if you dig deeper to find more than one solution, you can decide which one among them is less expensive than the others, or more durable, or more elegant—whichever outcome matters most to you. Second, and perhaps more significant, when problem-solving gets really hard and the way ahead isn't clear, you need to be ready to try anything. And the first step of the "try anything" approach is to back up and examine a problem from every angle, or at least from more angles than you can initially see.

In the real world, of course, we often resort to looking at problems from fresh angles out of desperation. "Try anything" is the motto. As one member of a two-working-parents household with elementary school twins during the COVID-19 pandemic, we often were compelled to try anything in order to solve problems with work, social distancing protocols, on and off remote school, and limited childcare. I will never forget one of my son's problem-solving victories focused on preventing us all from getting COVID.

One morning during the Omicron wave, my husband tested positive. The morning-person twin who was up with my husband freaked out and jumped into action. It was a crucial time at work for me and one of my sons had an important school project. Thinking quickly, our early-rising son basically pushed his dad (my husband) out of the apartment, assuring him he would toss into the hall anything he needed for the next ten days of social distancing. My other son and I groggily joined the problem-solving. We ran around the apartment, gathering his things and throwing them out the front door. I jumped online to find him a place to stay. It was both comedic and effective. The three of us did not get COVID that day. True problem-solving is dynamic and inclusive, just like that frantic morning. Think about being locked in an escape room (or imagine being trapped in one in real life). To get out, you hope that your teammates will come together and build on one another's ideas—the synergy of collaboration.

When you're open to multiple approaches, an answer can come to you from an unexpected direction. Probably the most famous breakthrough problem story is that of the ancient Greek scientist and mathematician Archimedes, who ran naked through the streets of ancient Syracuse in 300 BCE shouting "Eureka!" translating roughly as "I have found!" Archimedes had been ordered to find out if the crown of the king of Syracuse, who had given a goldsmith a bar of pure gold to work with, did in fact contain all that gold. The crown was an odd shape, so he couldn't weigh it on a scale against a matching pure gold item for reference, to make sure it wasn't silver with gold plating. If Archimedes was wrong, the king might kill him.

He puzzled over the problem for days, unable to solve it. He was willing to try anything. Then he went to take a bath. As he settled into the bathtub, he noticed that the water rose. That displacement matched the volume of his own irregularly shaped body. He wondered if water displacement could tell him something precise about an object. Checking equal masses of gold and silver, he found that the silver would displace more water, because it was less dense than the gold. He could now determine if the crown was gold: If it displaced the same amount of water as a pure gold bar, then he knew that the craftsman who had made it had not added silver to it. Eureka!

To expose the myth of a single correct method for the sham that it is, we need to understand the consequences of answer-getting versus problem-solving. Because we've been brainwashed into believing that answer-getting is good and because most of us spent years in answer-getting math curricula, we don't realize the negative effects it has on us.

Here are typical ways we respond in an answer-getting environment:

- Mind goes blank. For a moment, nothing occurs to us because we're not allowed to use our minds creatively.

- Second-guessing how to start (or whether to start at all) when confronted by a difficult math problem.

- Feeling defeated before even attempting to work on a problem.

- Racing heart. We react anxiously as we try to remember how the teacher did the math on the board; what was her first step?

- Negative self-talk. For a moment, we have the germ of an idea, an instinct about how to start solving a challenging math problem. But because we've been conditioned to seek the answer one and only one way, we chastise ourselves for thinking we know better than what we've been taught, and we revert to standard operating procedure.

- Reluctance to talk through questions and concerns with others. Embarrassed to bring up these issues, assuming they're "right way" adherents. This reluctance to involve others is an obstacle to a creative, collaborative process.

The overarching effect of an answer-getting system is disempowerment. Here are recent conversations I have had with children and adults on what this sort of math feels like:

"I want to use decimals. The teacher wants me to use fractions for no reason. I just have to do what he says. There is no freedom to do the math the way you want to do it, even if my way is easier for me. No one listens to me."

"I actually remember getting dinged on a high school math test even when I had the right answer, but I had solved it my own way. As a teenager, that made me furious. Now looking back as an adult, I think about it like tennis. If you are drilling me so I learn or improve a new skill like backhand volleys, then I can understand the reasoning for forcing a specific approach. But if you have no reason whatsoever for forcing your way on me, it still steams me to think about it."

A problem-solving approach conjures significantly contrasting responses—responses that reflect a sense of empowerment and courage. Ideally, schools would teach math with problem-solving as its driving principle rather than the myth of a single right way. To approach this ideal, however, we need to understand what problem-solving is all about.

Lost Keys and Writer's Block

Before homing in on what problem-solving in math looks like, let's spotlight some general principles by using everyday examples, starting with losing your car keys.

You get up in the morning and are getting ready to drive your children to school before heading to work, when you realize you can't find your keys. This is a problem, in that you don't want your children to be late for school, and you have a meeting scheduled that you can't miss.

To solve the problem, you use exploratory techniques—ones that may result in false leads and dead ends initially. Note that these false leads and dead ends aren't wrong or bad. They are how we expect to solve the problem of finding our keys. We use "retrace your steps" techniques, of which there are two types.

In type 1, you close your eyes and try to remember the exact place you were when you had your keys. Your train of thought goes like this: "I was walking into my apartment yesterday evening. What was I wearing? My blue raincoat. It was raining. Oh yeah, and I was carrying groceries and an umbrella. It was a treacherous entry into my slippery hallway actually. No wonder my keys slipped my mind. The keys are not in the drawer where I normally leave them, they aren't in my purse, but maybe they are in my raincoat pocket. Or maybe the grocery bag?!? Are they on that shelf near where I hang up the umbrellas?"

In type 2, you physically retrace your steps, moving around your home in search of your keys. To do this effectively, you merge your mental retracing with your physical experience. When you go to your entryway, you open the door. You try to move in chronological order. As you walk through the house, you may look to others like a mime—

but the concrete movement and experiences help you focus on the previous day. You see yourself put down the groceries. Remove your wet boots. Hang up your coat. Hang up the umbrella. Then, BAM! You found your keys on the shelf next to where you hang the umbrellas.

Many variations exist on these problem-solving techniques, depending on your personal preferences or the specifics of your challenge. One person might request help, asking her spouse if he recalls what she did with her keys. Another might spend a lot of time exploring the family room where she did stretches and other exercises before going for a walk, suspecting that those movements might have dislodged her keys from her pocket. Still another individual might use pen and paper to list other places she's lost keys and other objects in the past and focus her search on those places.

The point is that problem-solving involves experimenting and creativity, and it can be highly individualistic. There is no right way, but there are a variety of techniques likely to yield a positive outcome.

In another example, let's look at writer's block, which every member of my family has experienced and handles their own way. One of the twins gets angry at the rest of us. The other feels defeated, lamenting that he has no interesting ideas. I eat snacks.

Brain science research suggests another approach: Relax, lower the stakes, and free yourself. If you're stuck on a particularly tricky puzzle, consider some downtime—walking in nature, meditating, and other activities that allow the mind to relax and wander. Another approach that has worked for my family is to start wherever you can. All of us get overwhelmed when we have to write that first word or sentence or paragraph of a school essay or (in my case) a book. Instead of obsessing and stalling on those initial words, we have given ourselves permission to begin with anything—a random thought, a bunch of relevant words not even structured into a sentence, a concluding paragraph. Anything that primes the pump is okay.

There's no single right way to write. Some people listen to music, and others can't get a coherent thought out while music is playing. Some like writing in coffee shops with lots of words buzzing around them while others prefer monk-like silence and isolation. It is a path we have to find on our own. While we can use techniques like "Start wherever you can," we need to discover what works well for us within that general framework, whether that's free-associating words on a page or a more structured approach.

When kids struggle with writing in middle school, teachers are usually encouraging, suggesting some of these methods to help them overcome their blocks. Our academic approach is inclusive, and everyone is expected to find a way past their blocks and learn to write.

Our approach to math is exclusive. We let children opt out. If they can't solve a problem, they can't solve problems, and we comfort them by saying, "Well, you're not a math kid." They still have to take math, but they are told directly or indirectly that they just have to get through class and no one expects them to like or do well at it.

In the 1990s, MIT professor Mriganka Sur found that half the human brain is focused on vision. David Knill, also a professor of brain and cognitive sciences, asserts that "when scientists back in the 1950s met to talk about artificial intelligence, they thought that teaching a computer to play chess would be very difficult, but teaching a computer to see would be easy." In fact, it turned out that we could teach computers to beat chess masters, and that, contrary to appearances, teaching sight is incredibly difficult because vision is such a complex yet critical process.

To solve problems in math, we need to synchronize our approach with how the brain works—by visualizing the problem. We intuitively want to solve problems a certain way, whether it's finding our keys, overcoming writer's block, or dealing with a challenging school assignment. But when we are taught a rigid, abstract process as the only way, we sabotage our intuition. Maintaining and enhancing our intuition as we learn math requires using visualization techniques, like acting out the problem in our minds.

Consider this math problem.

> **Fold a 6-inch by 6-inch piece of paper into 4 equal parts. What is the area of 1 of the 4 parts?**

If you start by racking your brain for a formula and trying to decide if you should multiply or divide, you might drive yourself a bit nuts. But what is the first step? What's the right way to do this?

Now think about the lost keys and writer's block approaches. Perhaps you need to move the folded paper around a bit, turning it and looking at it from every angle. Maybe you can retrace your steps and go through the process of folding it into 4 equal parts. Maybe you should avoid focusing on the answer to the question and start with an easier calculation.

Try the following:

- Grab a piece of paper and roughly chop off the bottom so it's a square (or close to one), or just picture doing so. How do you fold it to get to 4 equal parts?

- Fold it (in your mind, if required) and you quickly know you need to fold it twice.

- After folding your paper in real life or in your mind, what is the area of one of the smaller parts? How would you calculate it?

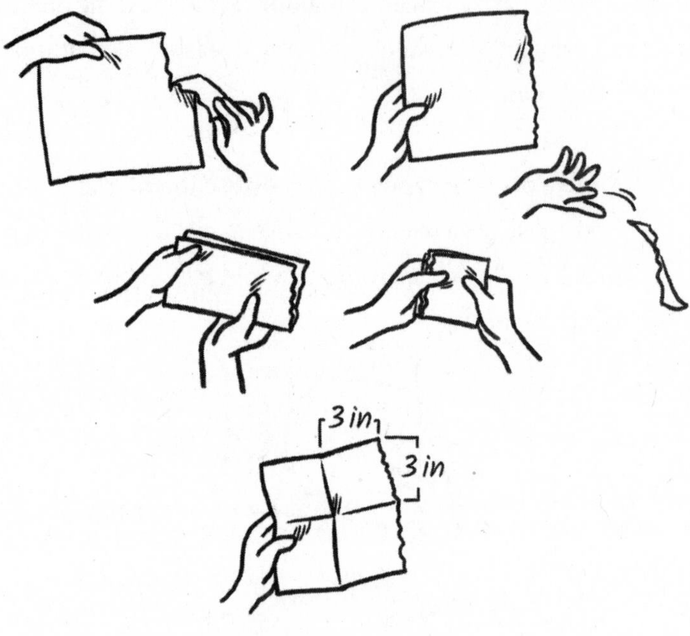

- Notice that one smaller square has 3 inches on each side length. So the answer is 9.

- Or observe that the side length of the big square is 6. And 6×6 is 36. And then one of the smaller squares is exactly $\frac{1}{4}$ of the bigger square. 36 divided by 4 is 9.

There's no formula, just pure human ingenuity. This is what math learning should develop, not the ability to regurgitate right answers.

How to Counteract the Myth

"Once you do know what the question actually is, you'll know what the answer means."

—DOUGLAS ADAMS, *THE HITCHHIKER'S GUIDE TO THE GALAXY*

We make math a performative rather than a learning experience. When the teacher asks the class, "What is the answer to 63 plus 37?" he turns math into an individual sport. Add the myth of speed, and each student is scrambling to come up with the answer first and win the game. The answer becomes the only thing that matters, and both understanding and collaboration fall by the wayside.

No doubt, some of you might wonder if I've lost my math mind. After all, we need to get the answers right so that we can purchase the right amount of carpeting to cover a room's floor or make sure that our rocket makes it to the moon. Again, this is an issue of integrative complexity. Of course, we need to know what 52 + 48 equals. But if that's all we know, then we're missing out on a lot of what math offers.

Fortunately, we can learn in a way that we obtain precision as well as other benefits. Consider again 63 + 37. What if the teacher framed the question this way: "Don't tell me the answer. It's 100. How would you start calculating

63 plus 37 in your head? What is your first step?" Now math is a process. I have gotten the chance to hear second graders' brains working at this moment many times. Each time is a joy. One might say, "I broke this up as 60 plus 30 plus 3 plus 7. And the next thing in my head I saw was that it was 93 plus 7. And then I knew that was 100." Another second grader might offer another option: "I looked at this for a moment, and I saw that 3 and 7 make 10. So I knew I had a 60 plus 30 plus 10. And I know that's 100."

This is the math people need in their lives. This is what is needed to build bridges. It's also how you build a math mind. Math should be taught as a collaborative process, much as other subjects are taught. We often view math as distinct from other subjects in K–8, as something that must be taught as an individual sport where everyone is on his or her own to come up with the right answer first. Other subjects are taught as team sports, ones where process matters, where students don't rely on tricks, where students are encouraged to work together, where a variety of ways to the answer may be acceptable. But when it comes to math, collaboration and process work are subordinated or eliminated.

The Joy of Math Making

Ask a random sampling of high school kids what they think about math, and you'll receive answers like these:

"Oh, I'm not good at math. But I think I am smart at other things." And: "I don't like math, and math doesn't like me."

Contrast these responses with what younger children tell me when I ask them what they like about math.

A second grader named Brayden told me, "I like division."

"That is wonderful," I said. "Why?"

"Because there is a *d* in division and a *d* in my name." I grinned and he skipped away.

Another child told me, "I love the number 8 because it is curvy and pretty."

These answers reflect an innocent, creative, and fearless perspective—a perspective we would be wise to nurture all the way through high school. These kids haven't learned to be intimidated or humiliated by their math work. They haven't yet bought into the myths of math and the idea that math is a losing struggle.

Here are two responses of older kids who have retained the brio of their younger cohort:

"I like that if you understand the concepts, you can learn anything. And math always makes sense; there is nothing illogical."

"In more advanced equations, I can solve it my way. There isn't one straight method. It is creative. And being creative makes you free."

These kids trust math. For them, math makes sense. They see the subject as empowering and as a gateway to learning. We need to help many more children develop this perspective, and the next section will suggest some of the ways for doing just that.

Part II

THE METHODS TO LEARN AND LOVE MATH

"What all beings consider as day is the night of ignorance for the wise, and what all creatures see as night is the day for the awakened."

—*BHAGAVAD GITA*, CHAPTER 2, VERSE 69

CHAPTER 5

Know You Belong

BELONGING MEANS FEELING LIKE A MEMBER OF THE club. Most of us feel (or have been made to feel) as if we don't belong in the math classroom, a demoralizing and isolating experience that we have come to accept quietly as normal. Popular culture tells us that math and feelings don't mix. Cutting-edge brain science shows us that feeling as though you don't belong interrupts the learning process itself, diminishes willingness to exhibit struggle, and reduces stamina and grit to persevere. In math, as in any learning pursuit, making mistakes is part of the learning process. However, in math in particular, we see mistakes as evidence that we don't have what it takes. We see them as proof that we don't belong in the world of math rather than as evidence we are learning math. Thus, ironically, in the world of math, we don't get cutting-edge science.

We approach math learning as if there's not enough of it to go around—a scarcity mindset that causes us to ignore belonging and to therefore make learning math much harder than it needs to be. What do I mean by scarcity?

Here's a true story of math hazing. On my first day of high school, I along with many of my classmates had math first period. This time, I made it into class a bit early. When I arrived, there were a few seats left. I took out a fresh notebook and looked around the room. I remember feeling alert and nervous. The desks were ordered in an almost perfect grid of four rows of five desks each. Strangely, there were a couple desks missing from the center.

As more students entered, the two missing desks became a problem. There were twenty students enrolled in the class but only enough desks for eighteen. My friend was one of the unlucky two standing, and I felt small and sad for her. With an incongruous smile, the teacher, Mr. Rockhill, announced that his class was rigorous. He told us that his honors math class provided our only path to AP Calculus BC. At least two of us, he said—but probably more—wouldn't make it. His words were received with pin-drop silence. He then walked out of the classroom and came back with the two missing desks and chairs.

Listening to him, my whole body tensed and my brain flooded with questions: Did he already know which two students he would cut? Was I one of them? That morning, Mr. Rockhill insisted that few students really had the ability to learn ninth-grade math (scarcity!), and that some number of us did not belong in his classroom. My friend was cut from the class once the second semester began. I was sad to see her go. I know it is irrational, but to this day, I wonder if her bad luck with the chairs somehow sealed her fate.

If math learning resources were limited or math weren't vital, perhaps Mr. Rockhill's approach would have made sense. However, in today's world, everyone can succeed in math learning. With billions of us who are numerate and literate, as well as education technology to complement the work of teachers, we don't need to operate with a scarcity mentality.

Yet we still do, deferential to tradition, arrogance, and elitism. If a part of you is holding on to the idea that math instruction should be rationed out to the most "gifted" students, consider this: It is in fact students with the highest working memory, the ones with the raw power who you'd expect to see thrive, who fall down the hardest when they feel they don't belong. Because those individuals have such high working memory, they often solve problems in more complex ways. They may be nearly simultaneously estimating the final answer and solving the math problem; they often rely heavily on mental math; and they often don't bother learning shortcuts because they don't need them. When stress sets in, and their working memory is impaired, their more complex problem-solving processes break down. So feelings of belonging are necessary for every student.

This is what happened to my brain for the rest of that math class and many classes to follow. I couldn't stop thinking about whether I was in the wrong class. Any careless mistake on a single homework problem alone at my desk became a high-stakes assessment of whether I would be worthy to study calculus three years later. Claude Steele, the celebrated Stanford psychologist, has referenced this as *churn*, when you are distracted from the task at hand (math) by worrying if you are confirming a stereotype (girls can't do math). Others call this math anxiety, being unable to perform under pressure. Still others talk about the biological effect of this hazing, fight or flight, blood leaving your brain, moving to your body to prepare you to run.

These explanations share one common feature: They mean that your working memory, literally your brain processing, is diminished by the stress of the way math is presented. Not to overstate the obvious point, but both learning and doing math require lots of working memory. Why would we actively engage in behaviors that diminish working memory?

I don't remember exactly when I settled into ninth-grade math to focus on the enjoyment of learning. What I do know is that it was after the second semester had begun, once the other students had been cut. I comforted myself with the feeling I had made it. The word on the street in my high school was that the next big cut wouldn't come until eleventh grade. I had scraped by.

Once I calmed down, I loved the math I learned that year. Hazing aside, Mr. Rockhill was an amazing teacher who worked very hard to make the math make sense for each of us who remained. Reading research and studying the Zearn web application analytics as an adult, I know now that the way back from this hazing or a sense of alienation—of not belonging—must include the experience of succeeding at math. I will share more about this in the coming chapters.

When kids are behind in middle school math, conversations about them often have a subtext: the assumption that it is too late. I know this is untrue. First of all, Zearn has billions of math problems completed on our platform that prove that middle school students who struggle with math can vault ahead to do grade-level math and dramatically improve their performance. I also love to share that Roger Federer first picked up a tennis racquet at age twelve, and Misty Copeland put on her first ballet shoes at thirteen, which is considered five to seven years past peak to achieve even a modicum of success in those fields. Adults can succeed and belong in math, too, even if childhood math was traumatic. Julia Child learned to cook at age forty. Suzanne Collins published *The Hunger Games* at forty-six. We all possess the capacity to master the key elements of mathematics. It's an incremental process—one of trying, failing, and then succeeding over and over again. At a certain point, an epiphany occurs: I can do this! I'm a math kid (or adult), too! I belong!

While schools can make kids feel like they don't belong in any subject—kids who learn to read more slowly may never learn to love reading, children who struggle in gym class may come to hate exercise—the sense of not belonging is a much more pervasive problem in math. That is because in general we approach these other areas by assuming there are abundant opportunities to achieve in them. Our society has on-ramps back for people who get detoured in many subjects. In other areas, we normalize later blooming so much that we do not notice it at all.

When one of my twins began reading before the other, friends and experts all reassured me that there was nothing to worry about. Kids learn to read at different ages, they insisted, telling me to stay calm and keep reading books to them. Their advice was based in abundance; in fact, they were so relaxed, so abundant in mindset, that they were telling me that my worries were not even real problems. Today, in seventh grade, you'd be hard-pressed to guess which of the twins read later.

We also offer children an abundance of reading experiences—libraries that encourage them with options like summer reading contests. Graphic novels, a genre that wasn't really around when I was a kid, provide on-ramps and enjoyment for students learning to read. Public health messaging is calm and constructive: Read to your child for twenty minutes a day. When children feel excluded in math because of a false sense of scarcity, however, they rarely receive subsequent experiences that foster a sense of belonging or abundance. To add to this, movies and the media depict math success as available only to the lone genius, who is also often depicted as an oddball. Those oddballs are also almost always white and Asian men. This is one reason our family has watched the movie *Hidden Figures* so many times. To see that, all along, there were women and people of color, albeit in the shadows, solving the most interesting math problems is important. But *Hidden Figures* is an anomaly in how we tell stories. For children, with most of the stories they encounter, the message of their exclusion from the world of math compounds.

Kids are more perceptive than they get credit for. They hear the implicit and often repeated message that they don't get it, don't have what it takes, and therefore, the community won't invest in them and include them. With regard to their math learning and struggles, they become isolated, don't seek help, and struggle more. Eventually, this vicious cycle becomes a self-fulfilling prophecy. The older the children are, the more attuned they are to these messages. Based on being told repeatedly they are outsiders in math, they make the seemingly rational decision to not invest in math.

But math can be taught in an inclusionary way. When this happens, kids are much more willing to make mistakes, display resilience, and try a new approach to solve a problem. I can't offer false promises. True belonging isn't possible without actually working the problems and getting correct results. But, like reading or soccer, kids pick up some parts of math at varying speeds. Learning at different speeds is no reason for anyone to be ostracized. And similar to any field, the late bloomers can develop into stellar math kids.

Contrasting Classrooms

Here is the typical exclusionary way that math is taught—the way most of us learned it. The teacher asks, "What is

251 plus 49?" As two or three other students' hands shoot up (the hands of the first-class citizens, the "math kids"), you haven't even finished processing the question. There is one problem, with only one answer, and the math kids are getting there first. Now your heart is pounding and your brain has stopped working; the blood has rushed to your legs so that you can be ready to run from a lion on the savannah. All you want to do is disappear. You pray for only one thing—not to be called on. You don't belong here.

Now contrast this approach with the following one. Instead of asking the question, the teacher writes these three questions on the board:

Instead of opening by asking for the answer, the teacher says, "Don't start with the answer, we will get there. Please, no hands shooting up or shouting out answers. Let's read these equations together. We are looking for the sums of 251 and 59, 251 and 49, and 251 and 39. Everyone take sixty seconds, look at all three equations, and then I'd like to hear three ways people started this problem. And I am interested in false starts, meaning you started one way but then went in another direction."

In a math classroom where belonging is cultivated, here are some likely responses:

Student: "I looked at the problems without the ones place numbers. That makes it friendly for me. So I saw 250 plus 50, 250 plus 40, 250 plus 30. And those I can do in my head, so I only had the ones left to work with."

Teacher: "Thank you! Who else would like to share?"

Student: "I started by seeing that in each problem the second number is going down by 10 each time—59, to 49, to 39."

Another student: "I did something different. I started with the ones place and saw each one had 9 plus 1 in the ones digit, so I added those across all three problems. That's 10. And then I saw the problem as 250 plus 50 plus 10; 250 plus 40 plus 10; 250 plus 30 plus 10. And then I could solve those in my head."

Teacher: "Great! Did anyone else notice this? What does this mean will happen to the answers?"

Another student: "It means you can check your answers across all three problems, each one should be 10 less than the one before."

Another student: "I stacked 251 plus 59 using the standard algorithm. I added the ones place first and carried the 10. My final answer was 310, and then because I also saw that each number was 10 less, I didn't bother adding the next ones up. I knew they were 300 and then 290."

Math should be a team sport, but it's taught as a solo endeavor. In the first scenario, the teacher created a tense, exclusionary environment by setting up a winner-take-all competition for an uninteresting addition problem in which speed and the right answer are all that count. Every person for themselves, with nearly no learning to be had. The child who shouted out the answer already knew it, and once they shouted it, it was over. The others checked out and didn't try.

In the second scenario, the teacher communicated that she was interested in building everyone's mathematical intuition and problem-solving muscles. Accordingly, she asked students to share their thinking, their strategies, their approaches that didn't work. By doing this, students were actually learning the deep rules of numbers: 251 is composed of a 200, a 50, and a 1. Or that you can add numbers in any order and the final answer will be the same. There are also metacognitive learnings—lessons about learning—including the demonstration that others may solve problems in more efficient and intuitive ways, and that you can adopt those strategies for yourself. You can even learn to ask others how they solve math problems to get better at solving problems. In this way, no one is excluded and there is far more learning to be had all around.

Traditionalists might scoff at the abstract idea of collaborative rather than competitive math, complaining that it lacks rigor. That makes sense as a knee-jerk reaction—feelings are soft and sloppy, and math is hard and disciplined. Anyone who scoffs, however, probably has never held STEM jobs, built software, or cut complex datasets. As someone who has done these things, I know that this is how math is applied in the real world. In a classroom like this one—a classroom in which children are sharing problem-solving strategies, where shouting out the final answer isn't the only thing that makes you valuable (in fact, it makes you unhelpful), where kids are collaborating and learning from one another, where this experience will help them solve problems better the next time—they are being trained for future work in which methodical and collaborative problem-solving is important. And when done right, sneakily, a pedagogy of belonging in math leads to a more rigorous approach to problem-solving. Both the kids who lack confidence in their math skills and those who feel okay can participate in this belonging-centric method—a method that mirrors real-world STEM environments and trains them to succeed there.

The Benefits of Membership

Scientists have studied the value of belonging, and the value is immense, especially when it comes to math. It's easy to dismiss belonging as a nice but fuzzy concept offering little in the way of tangible benefits. In fact, the evidence is overwhelming that when people feel as if they belong, they find it much easier to excel, and to enjoy that at which they excel.

While many studies exist that illustrate the importance of belonging in math, I'd like to share the results of one that has startling implications for how math is taught and learned. The seeds of the first study were sown in 2005 when Larry Summers, the then president of Harvard University, set off a firestorm by saying or implying (there's debate on what was actually said) that girls were not as capable as boys in the fields of STEM due to their gender.

What he and his colleagues were talking about was the lack of participation of women in the STEM pipeline at the university level. The STEM pipeline is sometimes called "leaky," meaning that despite the number of women able to participate in STEM careers based on scores comparable to men's, too many drop out.

Carol Dweck, Aneeta Rattan, and Catherine Good are researchers who responded to Summers's suggestion by wondering why there was a lack of participation. Why didn't women want to pursue math-based disciplines? Could they uncover any factors scientifically that explained the reluctance? And if they could, could they use science to increase the participation of women in STEM fields?

They decided to start the study with one of the places the pipeline broke for women in the top echelons of STEM: women attending highly selective universities enrolled in math courses, who went on to participate in STEM majors and careers in lower proportion to their male counterparts. These women did enroll in math courses. And they had objective measures to show they were both good at math and interested in it, yet the broader societal data showed that they and other women like them did not go on to pursue careers in STEM.

The researchers focused on four things. First, they wanted to understand if these women felt they belonged in their university community overall. They wanted to isolate general feelings of exclusion from feelings of math exclusion. Here they found that even if individuals felt they belonged in general or in many other contexts (such as other classes, clubs, and communities), that general sense of belonging didn't give them a boost with belonging in their math classes. The broader cultural narrative on math is so corrosive that general inclusion did not carry through. For math, belonging is domain specific. Further research has even suggested that math belonging may be topic specific—you may feel you belong in geometry but not in algebra.

The second discovery was how fragile belonging is even for these top performers. This finding suggests how powerful the cultural narrative of scarcity is in the math world. Even these women who had an irrefutable and lengthy track record of academic and math success were still wondering if they belonged—if their version of Mr. Rockhill still reserved a desk or chair for them. Researchers designed a survey for these high-performing female math students, and for their male counterparts. A startling number of females, but not males, responded in the affirmative when asked if they agreed with statements like these: "I feel inadequate," "I wish I were invisible." Conversely, unlike their male counterparts, the women did not agree that "even when I do poorly, I trust the instructor to have faith in my potential."

The researchers also examined external factors affecting a woman's sense of belonging. When gender stereotypes came up, perhaps a passing joke about women's capacity in math, it had a material impact on women's sense of belonging in the broader math community. It was so strong that it got the researchers wondering how much it affected the broader problem of women's participation in elite STEM fields.

And finally, this sense of belonging, as measured by their survey, was predictive of a woman's intent to stay in math at the most competitive university level. Without the sense of belonging, women who had a track record of math success for more than a decade could still be easily pushed off the math path and made to feel math wasn't for them.

This isn't just a women's issue. Men in math programs did better on the survey, but men can also harbor similar feelings of exclusion. Students of color with fewer role models grapple with feelings of exclusion in math. And kids, especially adolescents, struggle with belonging. A leading researcher in the field, David S. Yeager, notes that adolescence is a time when children are asking themselves, sometimes multiple times a day, "Am I the kind of person who can (and will be allowed to) succeed in school?"

But I cite the research about these women here because it's the tip of the iceberg. If women attending top universities, and have placed in top classes, struggle with math because they feel excluded, how might other students feel if they were convinced they didn't belong?

What Creates Belonging?

Experienced teachers and the research are clear about the two key actions to help kids feel like they belong in math. We may not think in the research lingo, but we still have the same ideas.

- Foster a growth mindset (or tell kids that success is built from hard work and good strategies, not the limits of their innate talent alone).
- Mitigate stereotype threat (or be aware of the subtle and explicit messages our culture conveys about who is good at math).

Let's start with growth mindset, a concept created by Dr. Dweck. She defines growth mindset as the consciousness of individuals who believe their talents can be developed through hard work, good strategies, and input from others. It is the opposite of what she calls a fixed mindset, the perspective of those who feel their talents are innate gifts. The former group tends to achieve more than the latter, in large part because they put more energy into learning rather than just relying on their natural skills.

When parents and teachers encourage kids to develop a growth mindset—to work hard at math, to develop self-efficacy, to ask questions—they start to get it and begin to feel they may actually belong. Let me illustrate how belonging happens by sharing a bit of my own story.

For much of my life, I suffered from a fixed mindset about lots and lots of things, though I wasn't aware of it. At the tail end of high school and in the beginning of college, I admired what I perceived to be effortless genius in others. I was surrounded by friends who would brag about how little effort they put into everything—their grades, their extracurriculars, their outfits. *Oh, I didn't really work on that paper; I am stunned to have gotten an A. How do I manage to lead the Sustainable Food Initiative Club and carry my courseload? Actually, it's kind of easy and the whole thing is a yawn. I just woke up and found this perfect outfit in a pile on my floor.*

I was embarrassed about how hard I had to work at everything compared to others in my social circle. I saw my effort not as a sign of my discipline and stamina but of my limited competence. I even remember consoling myself about it. I remember thinking, "It's okay, Shalinee, you just aren't smart or particularly talented at really anything. Others are. But you are a hard worker, and while that's not amazing, it's what you got."

But as Dweck notes, when you cultivate a growth mindset, the world changes for you. I am not being dramatic. The world just transforms. Day becomes night, and night, day.

In the second half of college and in my professional experiences at Bain & Company right out of college, I was lucky enough to be surrounded by friends and mentors who helped me cultivate a growth mindset. I had a friend who called himself a "worker." At first, I was embarrassed for him, but I came to admire him. Soon I sought out friends who were "workers"; I had found my tribe. Now when I see a beautiful historical building or watch a spectacular Bollywood dance scene, I am awed by the thousands of hours of hard work and dedication that allowed me to witness such excellence. I feel so much gratitude to the individuals for how hard they worked and that I get to see the culmination of it. Instead of feeling that I am witnessing effortless genius, I am awed by their sweat, persistence, and determination. I am awed by stamina.

I'm not suggesting that a growth mindset is a panacea for belonging, or that anyone has a permanent growth mindset—Dweck makes clear that we're all a mix of growth and fixed. But fostering a growth mindset can be a tool parents and teachers can use to help kids feel included in math learning.

How do you foster a growth mindset? Praising someone's effort rather than the outcome or ability is one way, but Dweck makes it clear that just saying "Good effort" is insufficient. If a child fails a math test and you say "Good effort," this child may hear "Nice try, you can't do this." Or worse, "Don't worry, you are not a math kid."

Instead, if a child bombs a math test, a much better approach is to say, "Okay. Let's reflect on this. What is this teaching us? What did you not understand? What can we do differently next time?" Getting points deducted on a test due to a careless computational error may result in independent learning. A student may work more slowly or check over his work next time. But if the child has fundamental misconceptions and doesn't understand, mistakes are only the very beginning of learning. The next step in teaching and learning for this child is to try new strategies and to understand the math.

In this way, the focus of a growth mindset is not on outcomes or on some generalized effort, it's on the process of navigating specific challenges and helping select strategies to address the challenges—the definition of the learning process itself. And a growth mindset response communicates implicitly, "Of course you can do this. Yep, it's really hard. I believe in you and I will support you."

The second recommendation for creating an environment of belonging is to mitigate stereotype threat. Claude Steele found that when people were reminded of their identity stereotypes as women or as Black people just before experiencing a math challenge, they performed worse than if they were not reminded of this status. Why? Because they were reminded they were outsiders in the world of math learning. They were reminded they didn't belong in math. Even when white men were reminded that Asian men outperform them in math, their performance dropped. No group was immune.

Stereotype threat is like multitasking. In ninth grade, when I knew the teacher was going to fail students out of his honors class, I assumed he was going to fail all the girls, though he never said anything to indicate that was his intent. I was already well aware of the stereotype that girls are not as good as boys in math and science. While pushing through my homework, in my head I could hear the voices of adults in my community: "Huh, she likes math," a big question mark in their tone.

Steele noted that those experiencing stereotype threat could not focus solely on the math challenge in front of them; students like me were engaging in two or more tasks. They would be battling against confirming the stereotype about them and, in doing so, fail to focus on the task at hand. Many of us would experience a stress response that impaired prefrontal cortex processing, and would perform poorly.

The interventions here are also simple:

1. Reduce cues that trigger worries about stereotypes. For example, a girls versus boys team in a seventh-grade math lesson is not a good idea because it primes students to remember and follow the pervasive stereotypes about women and STEM.

2. Set high expectations for all students and tell them you believe in them. This, more than anything, is the most effective antidote for churn. When my sixth-grade math teacher told me that I could be as smart as the boys,

he was communicating this point, albeit in his own outdated way. In the midst of my poor performance and struggle, he didn't pity me and lower his expectations. He challenged me to try my very best and told me he believed in me.

3. Reference representation and role models. The research shows it matters unequivocally for adults and children to see success that they can relate to. It implicitly messages that we can succeed, too.

Over the course of the last decade building and refining Zearn, I have been in thousands of math classrooms. As of this writing, students have completed more than fourteen billion K–8 math problems on our learning platform. Across all that experience and data, I have reflected a great deal on who belongs in a math classroom and why—and what we can do to help every student belong.

We all deserve to belong. I'm particularly sensitive to this because I have often felt like an outsider. I grew up as the kid of immigrants in Buffalo, New York, and I had the stark realization when we visited India that I didn't belong there either. My orientation makes me acutely aware of a child or an adult who feels like an outsider. Though they don't say anything, the message comes through loud and clear in their body language. When you take the time to include them and tell them they belong, they become less tense and more at ease in a given environment.

Belonging needs to be continuously cultivated. As we dive into new topics, and other contextual factors change, students may feel their sense of belonging diminish. It's like a garden; we always need to tend to it.

Here are some cultivating, not coddling, suggestions:

- Test students more often, with lower stakes. Think quizzes. A common approach in math is to give students a high-stakes diagnostic test up front. These diagnostics are of dubious value; for example, for many of these exams, the same student will receive a different score when they take the same assessment on another day. Regardless, students know that the purpose of the test is to sort them. We see better learning outcomes and higher engagement for all students when they experience more frequent tests, with less pressure around the outcome—taking quizzes many times a week, to show them where in the material they need to focus their attention.

- Start with a friendly question. For example: "What is this problem asking us?" or "What do we know about this problem?" Students need to feel welcomed into a community of math learners at the outset. As your mother told you, first impressions matter. How we begin a year, a unit of study, and a day of instruction tells the learner if they do or don't belong. We've seen that kids are hyperaware at the outset of these cues—of instruction that includes or excludes.

- Help students recover from setbacks with focused support. When children struggle or experience a setback—which all kids will—at those exact moments, they require the extra effort and engagement of teachers, parents, and even peers to help them feel they still belong, they can learn, and they can do hard things.

What Does Belonging Look Like?

At work and in my travels, I have asked people about their experiences in the world of math. Many are reluctant to discuss it—who wants to revisit what felt like educational torture? The relatively few adults who felt they belonged as kids and sailed through math classes—typically white or Asian males—are oblivious to what their classmates went through: "Wait, Shalinee, are you implying that people feel like outsiders in a math classroom? Is that really true?" Me looking quizzical: "Um, yes. It's true."

Here are three examples that illustrate the "feeling" of belonging in math, told to me by people who had to scrounge and fight to belong:

- **Math teacher and a national thought leader on teaching math (white man, visually impaired):** "The first person who told me I belonged in math was my fourth-grade teacher. She would take me aside and give me extra challenges. I liked pleasing her, so I did them. She gave me a full packet of math problems to do over the summer. I did every one. Initially, I wanted to please her, but over time I began to enjoy the math itself. It's pretty remarkable that she invited me into the world of math, because as a kid I was diagnosed with a rare degenerative eye disease. And most people told my parents and me that because of my eyes, I wouldn't be good at school. But despite my disability, by being invited into the world of math, I learned the opposite. I learned I could be a good learner if I worked hard and applied the right strategies. It changed my life."

- **A doctor (Asian woman):** "As a child, in math, I often would struggle and then get into a negative self-talk loop, and then give up. It hurt me in math and in school in general. A seventh-grade teacher told me something that changed my life. She looked at me intently and only said, 'You can do hard things.' She told me everyone here in this room is doing hard things. Today, even as a doctor and researcher, when I am overwhelmed, when I shrink from challenges or feel I don't belong, I can hear her. I say to myself, 'I can do hard things. Everyone here is doing hard things.' "

- **A successful entrepreneur (Black woman):** "It's hard to be what you can't see. And it's lonely to be the only one of something. Whether people are actively bullying you or not, you just feel bullied, isolated, and lonely when you are the only of something. That's how I felt in honors math and through many advanced classes in high school. It was actually after school, when I had bosses and mentors at work who were Black and women that I could see myself as a leader. As a Black woman, I am relentlessly focused on my three kids and how to help them navigate the broader social narrative that tells them they won't succeed in STEM and the wealth creation it offers because they are Black. I am always thinking of how they can belong. In our family, we have a saying, 'Hard is good.' "

Belonging isn't just cognitive; it's affective. It's not just knowing how to solve a math problem; it's feeling like you are part of a math community of learners where every member is valued and can—no, must—contribute.

CHAPTER 6

Use Pictures and Objects

BELIEVING IN YOUR ABILITY TO LEARN MATH IS ESSEN-tial to learning math, but belief alone is not enough. The sense of belonging matters, but we can't change the feelings of mass alienation by greeting each other enthusiastically at the classroom door or by setting a goal that everyone should feel welcome. Ending hazing and bullying is only a starting point. The way to become comfortable with learning math is to, in fact, learn math.

Once in a meeting on math learning that I was attending with school superintendents of the largest cities (and school districts) in the country, one leader said, "Math is a language and we haven't taught it to all our kids." That is exactly right. No one would suppose that children would be able to understand a novel in Spanish just because their Spanish classroom was welcoming; they'd still have to know the Spanish language, no matter how inviting the classroom.

So, how do we continue the work of counteracting the pervasive math myths? What is the right method to teach the language of math so it makes sense and so that it isn't all about speed or tricks or doing problems one specific way?

The best approach begins by recognizing a singular reality: We are preprogrammed from birth to do math with pictures and objects. This is supported by the way math is taught in the highest-performing countries, and it's a core insight from Zearn's learning dataset of billions of math problems created by millions of children. Recognizing this reality guides the way to a superior alternative to the math most of us were taught.

To understand how this is so, I'm going to ask you to prove something to me.

A Picture Is Proof

Prove that 4 is bigger than 3. You may be thinking, "It's obvious." Yes, but how would you go about proving the obvious? I recognize this task feels as pointless as proving that the sun will rise tomorrow, a fun and famous philosophical discussion. But the proof exists if you just look around.

Grab 7 objects in front of you—pens, forks, cell phone charging wires, whatever—and separate them in two neat piles, one pile of 3 and one pile of 4. The evidence is right in front of your eyes—the pile of 4 has more items than the pile of 3; 4 is bigger than 3.

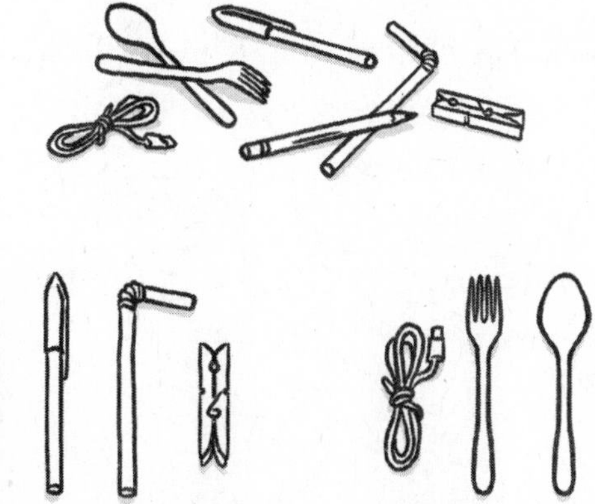

I asked you to prove the obvious because it leads you to this truth: Creating the piles provides a visceral understanding of the quantities associated with the symbols 4 and 3. These numbers are not simply symbols or hieroglyphs. They are quantities of which you possess absolute and concrete knowledge.

What about $\frac{1}{3}$ versus $\frac{1}{4}$? Which is bigger? Let's say the stakes are high. Someone is going to steal $\frac{1}{3}$ of your bank account balance, or $\frac{1}{4}$. Did you respond reflexively? Or did you pause for a moment to remember which number is bigger, to decipher what the symbols mean?

In sixth grade, my wonderful math teacher, Mr. Snyder, was frustrated with our class because we were obsessed with getting the right answers at the expense of deep understanding. He told us a story that illustrated the perils of learning math without understanding it, the tale of the A&W's Third Pounder. In the early 1980s, A&W launched a hamburger that tasted better, according to blind taste tests, and offered more meat than the McDonald's Quarter Pounder. Their advertising copy read, "A&W has bigger, better third-pound burgers." The slogan to promote the burger highlighted the quantity: "Third is the word."

Source: "Third is the Word" advertisement
© A&W Restaurants, Inc., 1980

The McDonald's Quarter Pounder offers, well, one quarter of a pound, or 4 ounces, of meat. This better-tasting and bigger burger, with $5.\bar{3}$ ounces of meat, was offered for the same price as McDonald's. Nevertheless, the product launch failed.

When the A&W's team investigated the failure, they discovered that most people believed the Third Pounder contained less meat than the Quarter Pounder because the number 3 is smaller than the number 4. Instead of seeing the better deal, they perceived they were being ripped off. To quote education journalist Elizabeth Green, "The Third Pounder presented the American public with a test in fractions. And we failed."

The Visual-Intuitive Connection

The story of Americans failing at fractions is a story of lost intuition. It's similar to not knowing if the sun will rise tomorrow or whether 4 is a bigger quantity than 3. (One area where I lament diminishing intuition is my sense of direction as I become more reliant on GPS.) Fortunately, regaining our intuitive sense in the case of fractions is possible by studying math through pictures and objects. This isn't about dumbing down the material. As someone who has worked in STEM fields for decades, I assure you that math pictures represent the height of rigor.

The concept of the quantity 3 or 4 was taught to you when you were so small you can't remember learning it anymore. Because you had limited capacity with spoken language and little capacity with the written language, you learned what 3 was versus 4 through concrete means, the only means you had. Your family taught you intentionally or accidentally with objects, and these were likely objects that mattered to you. As a toddler and young child, you learned the value of transitioning your shrieks of "more" to specific numbers: Three red blocks. Four round crackers. Two animal cookies. Five cheerios.

By the time you learned about fractions as numbers, however, you could read and write. Poor you. The luckier students—including the vast majority of kids in high-performing math countries such as Finland and Singapore—were able to experience fractions concretely, similar to how small children learn about whole numbers. Instead of being shown abstract and confusing symbols, with one digit stacked on top of another, they were slicing up oranges and cakes in class to learn about $\frac{1}{2}$, $\frac{1}{4}$, or $\frac{1}{3}$. They broke up crackers and cookies to share them. They made math pictures, lots of them! Rather than filling out a tiny space on a photocopied worksheet, they engaged in these concrete activities for years, not just in kindergarten, each and every day in math class, learning viscerally and deeply that $\frac{1}{3}$ is bigger than $\frac{1}{4}$. These kids would see and draw simple pictures like this all the time:

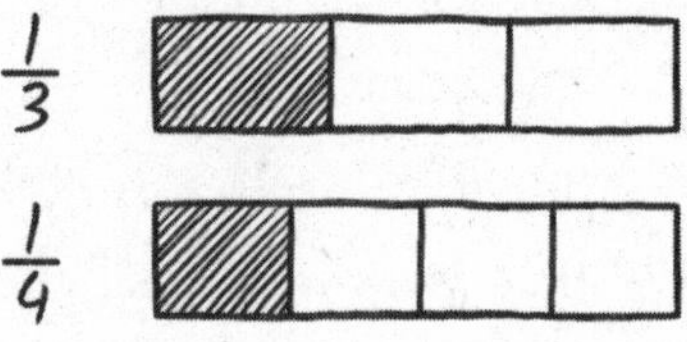

For them, fractions are real quantities that they understand concretely. Their understanding was built with pictures and objects. As humans, the majority of our experience in life is in the concrete world. The easiest way to learn something new is to attach your learning to something you already know. Because most of what we know is concrete, cutting-edge brain science shows us that it's easier to learn almost anything by starting with the physical world, no matter our age or sophistication.

These objects and pictures weren't just used in the introductory lessons on fractions and then dropped. Pictures and objects continued to be part of learning, especially at critical moments as concepts advanced.

For example, what is $\frac{1}{2}$? That is an easy one to grasp. You can picture a half-moon or half a pizza.

But what is $\frac{8}{4}$? What does it mean when the numerator is bigger than the denominator? We can memorize tricks to manipulate these symbols, but can a child have an intuitive understanding of that number (when so many adults may not)? What we have learned through years of trial and error is yes, they can and they must. Success in fractions in third through fifth grade is shown to be the biggest predictor of success in algebra. Success in algebra and one additional high school–level math class is the biggest predictor of graduating high school and college. So understanding what the symbol $\frac{8}{4}$ means has quite a bit riding on it.

We discovered that when we transitioned to a new, interesting idea inside the study of fractions—for instance, that fractions could represent not just numbers smaller than one, but a number bigger than one—we needed to return to the concrete. When we did, our students could once again understand fractions intuitively and deeply. How did we do it?

To make sense of $\frac{8}{4}$, we videoed one of our on-screen teachers, Mr. Sawicki, cutting up two oranges slowly as if in front of a classroom.

First, Mr. Sawicki cut one orange into fourths.

And then he cut the next orange into fourths.

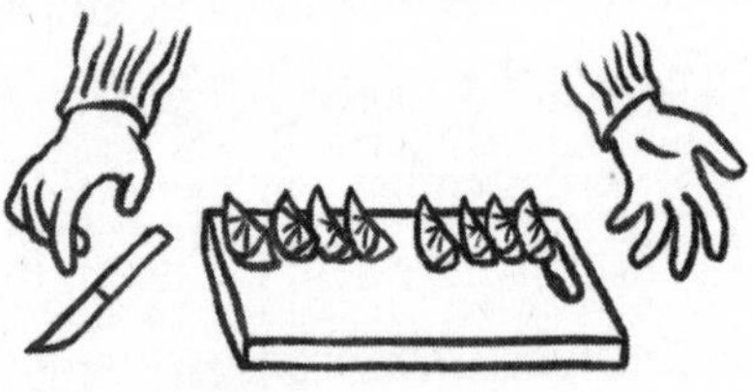

We utilize twenty-five seconds of video to show the entire experience of cutting up 2 oranges into 4 pieces each to represent $\frac{8}{4}$ as a real quantity. While it might seem like a waste of time to watch our on-camera teacher, Mr. Sawicki, slice up an orange by hand for twenty-five seconds, it is anything but. Another way to represent $\frac{8}{4}$ is 2. It might take weeks to explain to a young student abstractly, through worksheets, that $\frac{8}{4}$ can be reduced or simplified to 2. By cutting oranges, we have shown it to be true in a way that can be viscerally understood and remembered in less than half a minute.

Two oranges cut into 4 pieces each make 8 pieces. That's the meaning of $\frac{8}{4}$.

While drawing pictures might not seem like real math, real mathematicians draw pictures all the time. Even if you aren't working through equations, math pictures represent sophisticated mathematical thinking. Unfortunately, we don't recognize this truth because we've lost our way—it's like losing our musical sense. Any human can hum or tap out a rhythm even if they lack musical training and can't read music. But what if we learn the music in a way that takes away intuition and so we can no longer hum a tune or tap out a rhythm? This is what we are doing to our math intuition. Top-performing math countries strengthen their students' intuition. Drawing and using math pictures and concrete contexts is an intuition-fostering strategy; it is one key element for building numeracy.

If you're still skeptical, recall the birds and two-day-old babies doing math. What I didn't mention was how they learned math: The math was presented to them in concrete objects and pictures. They never saw a symbol like a multiplication, division, or equal sign. Instead, they were shown bowls of treats or red balls. Using interesting objects, they were comparing, adding, and subtracting. They were not memorizing rules or decoding symbols. They were making sense of the world they lived in.

Concrete to Pictorial to Abstract

People often ask me for the magical solution to teaching math. They want a reductive and easy answer that can be summed up in a sentence: "We need to make problem-solving relevant to kid's lives." Or: "We need to memorize up to our 25 times tables." These are slogans, not solutions. Transforming math education—creating new methods and structures to develop the reasoning mind—is a nuanced endeavor. Beware of reductive answers.

Still, the following serves as a guiding principle: "Everyone will be able to understand and do mathematics if we follow a progression from concrete to pictorial to abstract." Not billboard material, perhaps, but a truth that can help us figure out the best approach. To make all kids math kids, we must utilize a progression of concrete objects, math pictures, and abstract equations to build understanding and fluency.

As I mentioned earlier, we learn by connecting our new knowledge to what we already know. If we can't make that bridge, the knowledge won't stick. When new knowledge attaches to existing knowledge, you might experience a small eureka moment, a dopamine hit to the brain, an internal message that sounds something like this: "Oh! I get it; it's like when . . ."

The vast majority of what we know is by touching and seeing the world we live in. Therefore, the easiest way to access a new idea is to make it concrete or visual. What if you're not a "visual learner"? Don't worry at all, because there is no such thing. Research demonstrates that the popular ideas about separate learning styles—visual versus auditory versus kinesthetic—are fallacious. Every single one of us is a visual learner in addition to being able to learn in other ways. In fact, learning deepens when we can use multiple modalities or learn the same thing in more than one way.

So, when I'm asked to boil down how we could transform math education so we could all enjoy it and be successful, I respond along the following lines:

"Use mathematical pictures. The most accomplished STEM experts use these pictures in daily conversations and to formulate their breakthroughs (e.g., Watson and Crick's double helix or Mendeleev's periodic table of elements). They are a simpler and more elegant way to understand the core math ideas versus only abstract symbols and mathematical notation, and these same pictures are the best way to teach kids, too!"

Bringing visualizations into math teaching and learning is the single most impactful change we could make. If done right, it would make math more accessible to more people and simultaneously more rigorous. Other efforts to expand numeracy tend to take an either-or approach—either dumbing down the standard itself (who even needs algebra?) to achieve wider numeracy or finding avenues to push numeracy that are currently interesting only to a small number of children and adults alike (for instance, math Olympiad competitions).

Where representations—the fancy word for math pictures—have entered instruction and become part of people's thinking, achievement scores improve quickly. Singapore provides a compelling example, with results far outpacing the US average. Yet they are not common practice. Today, the use of objects and images is either limited to the youngest kids or employed in only a specific context.

A few years back, I was chatting with a fabulously successful investor. He asked me what I had learned building Zearn, with our millions of students solving billions of problems. I said we discovered that pictures, especially brightly colored ones, helped students get the next question right when they got things wrong.

As an investor, remember, he is someone who does a lot of math and trades millions of dollars on his formulas. But at the mention of the pictures, he lit up. When he was a kid, he told me, he couldn't remember the difference between the greater than or less than signs until a teacher told him to think about each symbol as a picture of a mouth. Once he was able to envision the "hungry mouth" opening wide for the bigger number, it clicked. Using his hand, this guy with a PhD in pure mathematics mimed a hungry mouth snapping up a number. I smiled and tried to hide my astonishment. I thought, "Point made."

We know from brain science that thinking in symbols requires development of the prefrontal cortex that young children haven't gone through yet. That means that before kids can think about math in terms of *x*'s and *y*'s and even numerals, two things must happen. First, parts of their brain need to grow, specifically the prefrontal cortex. Second, once they have that physical capacity, they need to be taught that a symbol can have two meanings, or what is termed "dual representation"—that the object may be both itself and something else. When you see a map in a stairwell displaying the nearest fire exit, accompanied by a "you are here" red circle, your brain needs to activate your ability for dual representation. The map is a compact object made of paper with black lines and red markings, framed and hung on a wall. The map is also a picture that is showing you the larger layout of the building and your position within it. Toddlers can't understand both ideas. For them the world is far more concrete. They are not literally inside a map hanging in a stairwell, so for them the map is silly. They are not "here" from the map's point of view.

As part of building our digital lessons, we have gone to classrooms about once a week for ten years to hear what kids think and capture their thoughts on video. In one visit, we heard this feedback from a pre-K student on our kindergarten lesson in development. As she completed the lesson, a brain popped up on the screen and appeared to grow. The kindergartner asked her what was happening. A teammate replied, "That's your brain getting bigger because you have learned so much this year." The child replied with worry about the adult's comprehension: "Um, but my brain is inside my head." I laugh every time I watch this video.

One experiment in particular memorably demonstrates the process of learning dual representation. Three psychologists, Judy S. DeLoache, Kevin F. Miller, and Karl S. Rosengren, were trying to understand how children develop abstract thinking, working with toddlers aged two to three. In the experiment, they showed a two-and-a-half-year-old girl a dollhouse. Then, with the little girl's help, they hid a miniature teddy bear underneath a sofa in the dollhouse. They walked the little girl to a (real) door and asked her to open it. On the other side was an exact replica of the dollhouse room. They asked her to find the teddy bear, which in the big room was also hidden under the sofa. The toddler couldn't find it, and neither could any of the other toddlers who went through the same steps. The researchers proceeded to connect the dots by telling the toddlers that the researchers had magical abilities and could shrink and grow rooms, transporting objects from the dollhouse to the real room. The researchers made sound effects to indicate rooms were growing and shrinking, and finally the toddlers understood the dollhouse room and real room were representations of each other. They could find the teddy bear.

It's no accident that math presents in base 10 and we have ten fingers. I share this story as a concrete example of how our brains work and develop. While the prefrontal cortex is still growing, the ability to work with symbols and dual representation needs other forms of support. Think about complex equations from algebra. In sixth grade, when learning ratios and proportional reasoning—a big idea needed for algebra—students can better understand the concept if it begins with a concrete or pictorial start. Imagine making peanut butter and jelly sandwiches. Some are 1:1 peanut butter to jelly in the sandwiches, others are 1:3, and still others are 3:1. In the first the amount of peanut butter to jelly is equal, for every one teaspoon of peanut butter, you use one teaspoon of jelly. And in the other sandwiches, there is more jelly or peanut butter. Students can decide what kind of sandwiches they like.

Peanut butter and jelly are objects that facilitate our grasp of ratios, and while the amount of one condiment versus the other may seem trivial, ratios matter because they help us think about the world around us.

Experimentalists have been demonstrating the value of concrete learning for longer than we have had brain science to support it. Years ago, before there were MRI machines to track brain function, child development experts tested theories about teaching by working with children directly in a scientific way. These experimentalists include Maria Montessori and psychologist Jerome Bruner. The Montessori method and schools come from her work. In working with children, pediatrician Montessori created her famous wooden teaching objects that you can still find used (and misused) in classrooms today—with the goal of building a concrete understanding of abstract concepts in a fun, accessible way. As Bruner noted, "We begin with the hypothesis that any subject can be taught effectively in some intellectually honest form to any child at any stage of development." Both concluded that concrete learning was essential, especially for young children, children with learning differences, and children learning new things.

Though Bruner was a Harvard professor, Singapore, not the United States, is one of the nations that embraced his work. His concrete to pictorial to abstract model has helped that country's children master mathematics, and it is where "Singapore Math"—a phrase that is uttered with admiration and approval by educators and parents in the know in the US—is just called math. In that country, when a new idea is introduced, even in sixth grade, it begins with action or manipulation of concrete materials, then moves to representations or math pictures, and finally ends with abstract symbolic equations, those standard equations you remember when you think back to middle school math. The result is that kids know both what is happening and how to do the math itself. They understand viscerally and they can compute proficiently.

But long before the Singapore curriculum was born, concrete objects and symbolic visualization fostered history-changing breakthroughs. Legendary scientific discoveries revolving around physical or visual insights include Isaac Newton being hit on the head with an apple, James Watson dreaming of a spiral staircase that led him to the double helix of DNA, and Dmitri Mendeleev dreaming of the periodic table of elements.

When you stop thinking about math in abstract, recondite terms, the link between these images or objects and math makes sense. Math is simply a language to describe our physical world. Without a picture, scientists struggle to find the pattern; the rest of us will struggle at least as much. Bridging that connection to pictures makes math easier to understand for all humans and unexpectedly makes it more rigorous as well.

When we train teachers, we show them pictures—ratio examples like the peanut butter and jelly sandwiches, or other food items like making bags of trail mix or a glass of chocolate milk. They respond: *Wow, I wish I had learned math like this. If I had, I would have been good at math. I have to give this to my kids.* Understanding is visceral. Understanding is always concrete. Once we understand something concretely, only then can we abstract from it.

Pretzels and Cubes

The odds are that you did some story problems when you were in school—problems that were sometimes referred to as brainteasers. They can seem daunting when we have only abstract tools, *x*'s and *y*'s, to work with. Once you utilize pictures as well, even if only in your mind, they become much more comprehensible.

Let's do a couple of story problems together.

Connor and Lily are making bags of trail mix. Connor puts 7 pretzels in each bag, and Lily puts the same unknown number of raisins, *r*, in each bag. After filling 3 bags, they have used 45 items. Solve for *r*.

This is a seventh-grade story problem that relies on a student being able to translate this word problem into an abstract equation, a core part of pre-algebra. For some who are fluent in the abstract language of math, they might pretty quickly start doing something like this on a piece of paper.

$$3(7 + r) = 45$$

$$21 + 3r = 45$$

$$-21 \qquad -21$$

$$\frac{3r}{3} = \frac{24}{3}$$

$$r = 8$$

But we know that, for seventh graders, one of the hardest things is turning this word problem into an abstract equation. It's even hard for higher-scoring students who became used to their mental capacity and never writing anything down. At some point, as you move into algebraic work, you do need to write down the equations to solve them.

That first step of turning this story problem into the equation $3(7 + r) = 45$ can be a challenge. There are also other key parts of this word problem, such as the mechanics of knowing how to simplify this equation to get to $r = 8$. I can't really overstate this. For many students, this is the exact moment when math no longer makes any sense, and they finally surrender. They endure the rest of the required classes, memorizing, guessing, groping in the dark, certain that math won't make sense because they don't have the ability.

Pictures and now, better, in-app GIFs can bring this to life. Let's look at this same word problem. Here's the movie in my mind: There are 3 bags. You can see Connor physically placing 7 pretzels in each. Lily is going to put in the raisins, and when all the bags are full, there will be 45 items. As I visualize the problem, I am quietly restating it to myself. I am understanding.

Connor and Lily are making bags of trail mix.

Connor puts 7 pretzels in each bag and Lily puts the same unknown number of raisins, r, in each bag. After filling 3 bags, they have used 45 items.

Solve for r.

Here's another image that visualizes the algebraic thinking required for this story problem.

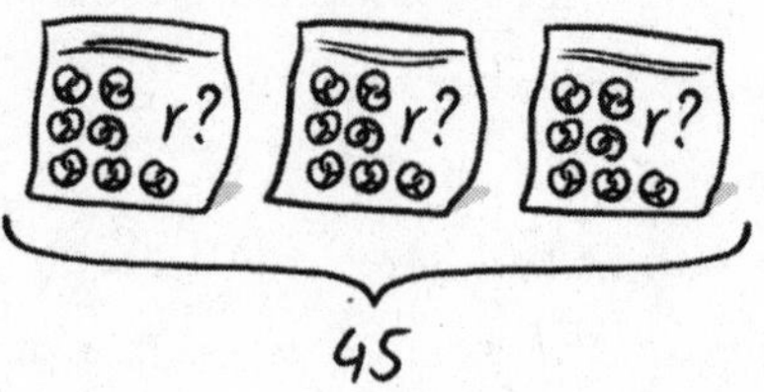

What these pictures offer is a scaffold or a way into learning how to build the equation that this problem describes, $3(7 + r) = 45$, when you can't see the equation immediately yet.

Here's another example:

> **A storage company has two options for storage: the "Cube" and the "Double." The Cube is a true cube and has a storage volume of 64 m^3. The Double holds double the volume of the Cube but takes the same footprint. What are the possible dimensions of the Double?**

Many will start solving this problem by determining the height, width, and length of the Cube. After guessing and checking, you will conclude it is 4, because $4 \times 4 \times 4 = 64$. But now what will you double to get twice the volume of the Cube while maintaining the same footprint? Is the correct size of the Double $8 \times 8 \times 8$?

Pictures turn this from a hard math problem to a simple concrete problem of imagining two cubes stacked.

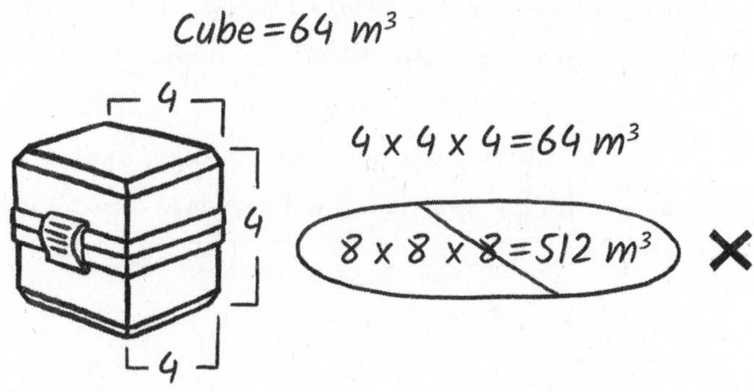

$8 \times 8 \times 8$ is 512 m³—far more than double 64 m³. It is, in fact, eight times the size, meaning that Octuple would be a more accurate brand name for this version. Further, this storage bin would not have the same footing as the cube because all three side lengths double.

Here's an octuple. When we see it, we instantly know $8 \times 8 \times 8$ is not double $4 \times 4 \times 4$.

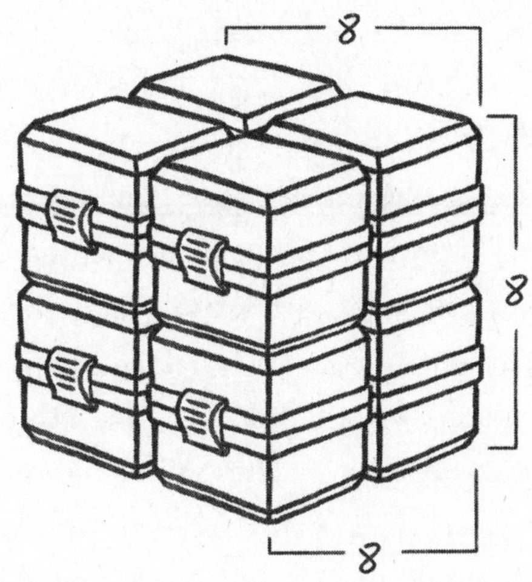

Pictures transform this abstract head-scratcher into a simple exercise. You can follow the visual logic: If you stack two cubes on top of each other to make a new shape, only one side length doubles. It becomes a rectangular prism. Or here's another perspective: The figure is just two cubes sitting on top of each other.

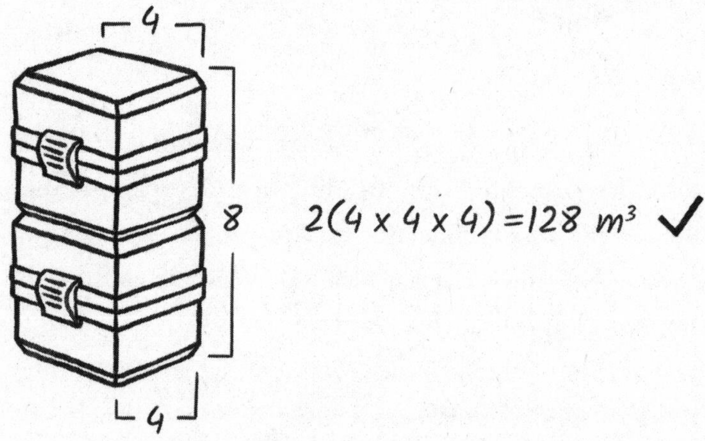

Why kids learn best by moving from concrete to pictorial to abstract can be understood best by "seeing" this progression. There's an "Aha!" moment that communicates the value of this method far better than any long-winded explanation. To provide this epiphany, let me share some visuals, moving from preschool to middle school. First, how do children even come to learn that the symbol 2 expresses the quantity 2, and that 2 itself is a thing. It starts with two apples. Apples are fruit to eat, and there are two of them. We can then draw two circles on a page. A drawing of a circle is a thing, and Mommy made two of them. And finally, there is just 2, because 2 modifying only itself is also a concept. It is 2.

And finally:

2

That's how we teach a preschool concept, but it's also how we might teach ratios and proportional reasoning, a sixth-grade concept that is one of the most vital building blocks of algebra.

We start with a ratio in a fruit bowl—1 banana to 2 apples. If that ratio is fixed and we have more fruit, then we might have 2 bananas and 4 apples. We can quickly move a middle schooler from fruit to 1 square to 2 circles. And then we can finally explain that the relationship of 1:2 is itself a concept. It's a ratio.

1:2

As our brains grow, we build our abstract math sense of symbols and numbers. As adults, we know the symbol 2 is 2, and a picture of two apples is certainly not required. However, at each stage of math exploration, when we haven't yet mastered the idea abstractly, we can understand complex ideas using pictures and objects. This means that whether you are in kindergarten or are a mathematician building AI algorithms, the easiest way to access or deepen your understanding of an idea is to make it concrete or visual. Ultimately, the acid test of whether you understand the math at all is if you can draw a picture.

CHAPTER 7

Make an Easier Problem

IN THE EARLY YEARS OF BUILDING ZEARN, I SPENT THOU-sands of hours observing students in math classrooms, and I noticed something startling. Students who enjoyed and did well solved problems in a dissimilar way than students who struggled. The most unexpected part was that successful kids seemed to be both "lazier" and unorthodox. That is, they often didn't start solving the problem immediately when it was presented to them. Instead, they stopped to consider it and try to understand it. And then with that pause and resulting insight, they usually looked for an easier way to do it.

Don't be discouraged if you or your kids have always found math difficult. You, too, can find an easier way, with a bit of help. Take heart if you haven't yet. Most successful math students—kids or adults—I have encountered over the last decade were *shown* different methods and mindsets, rather than just naturally finding them on their own. A small percentage do discover easier ways themselves, but the majority were taught, and then learned how to keep using them on other problems.

Yes, the powers that be kept the easier ways from you. They never told you that you were allowed to make a problem more accessible. This betrayal was not intentional, of course. And let me reassure you that easier doesn't mean shortchanging the work. As you'll discover, these easier methods translate to better problem-solving strategies in real life.

If you're asking yourself, "Is there really an easier way?" the answer is yes. But it does require a mix of questioning and patience. In this chapter, I want to examine one math problem from many angles to bring easier ways to light. I also want to show you that making an easier problem requires a mindset and a process. As you read, remember that the students who use these approaches were not necessarily born with superior skills. Instead, they were taught to look for and even demand an easier way.

The "demand" part is key. If you demand something, it means you consider yourself worthy. Is this particular math problem something you bend down to, barely understanding, hoping to remember the formula someone taught you? Or is it something you have the right or even authority to solve, to investigate, to understand?

Let's begin here.

$$35 \times 18 = ?$$

What is one way you could start this problem? Not complete it. Just start. Remember: No one is shouting out the answer the fastest. Focus on your first step.

A common response is to rewrite the equation stacked, so we can complete the multiplication algorithm. Like this:

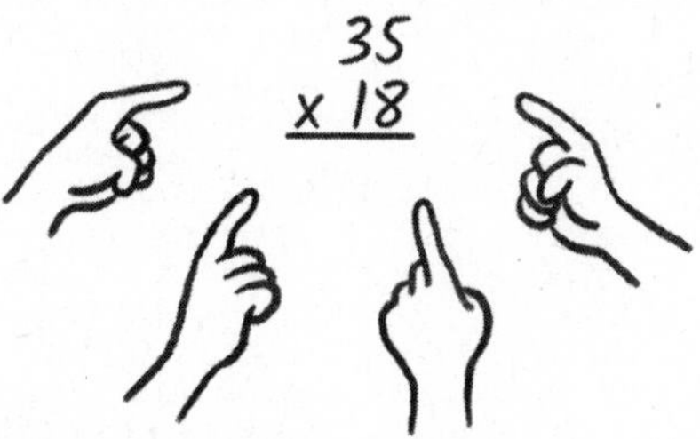

What is another way? Is there an easier way for you? I have presented this problem to hundreds of people and asked them how they would start and how they could make it easier. (This is the downside of inviting me to a dinner party.) The range of answers is highly diverse.

Many will utilize the conventional algorithm displayed above, as we were all taught to do in school. But many of us, even those who use it as a first choice, find the algorithm to be tedious. Those who were taught to hunt for an easier way try other strategies.

Here's one. Change the numbers to easier numbers. Some will change the number 18 to 20. So instead of solving 35 × 18, they are now solving 35 × 20. Here's a picture of the steps they may be taking in their head or on paper.

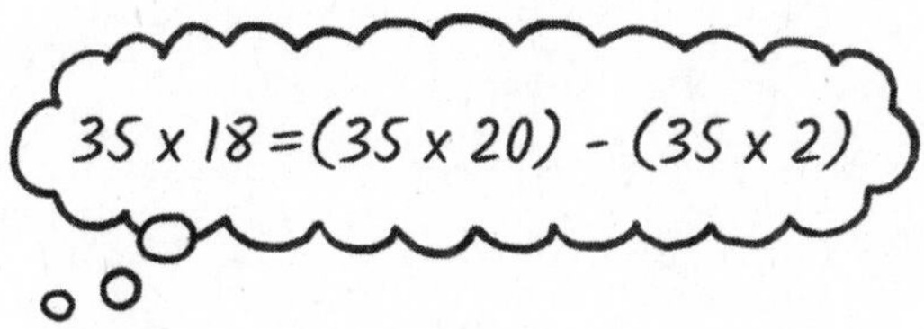

Now, you might be thinking, "No thought bubble like that has ever come out of my head." The illustrations are not intended to be literally what people are picturing in their minds. When I talk with kids and adults about how we might make an easier problem, I insist people verbalize what they are doing if they are solving in their heads. Few are picturing equations like the illustrations in the book. Many don't have any specific images in their head. But now we can see what's going on.

As a next step, many will verbalize their approach by saying something like "I want to change 18 to 20. I know 35 times 10 is 350. And then because it is 20, not 10, that we are multiplying by, I need two 350s. So that is 700." Others will say, "35 times 2 is 70, and because it is 20, not 2, I need to multiply now by a 10. So the total is 700." Here is an illustration of these trains of thought:

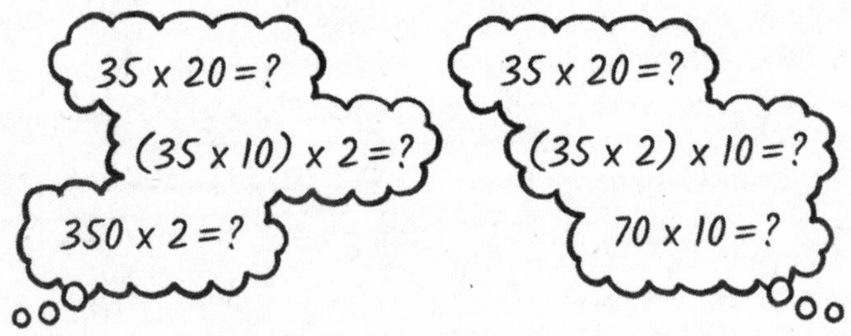

Now we have the answer to 35 × 20, which is 700. But we don't yet have the answer to 35 × 18.

At this point, there are fewer differences in what comes next. Here's an example of what you might hear when you talk to a middle schooler at this point in the problem.

"So, I know 35 times 20 is 700. But I am solving for 18 groups of 35. And so, I need to take 2 groups of 35 away. Or I need to take 70 away. Another way of saying that is 35 times 18 is the same as 700 minus 70." And here, we can conclude that the answer is 630.

I find this strategy easier than the algorithm, but that doesn't mean it works for everyone—or even for me! Easiness, like beauty, is in the eye of the beholder. Another middle schooler described a way to solve that I find harder, but she preferred. She decided to break the number 18 into an 8 and 10. She quickly multiplied 35 × 10 in her head. Easy: 350. Then she had 35 × 8. That's not as easy. At that point, she grabbed a piece of paper and scratched out a quick algorithm of 35 × 8 to get 280. She was then left with adding 350 + 280 to get to 630.

Not every attempt to make a problem easier will be fruitful in solving that specific problem. Further, sometimes easier is about personal preference and style. It's not a rote process to be copied. Instead, it is a mindset, and it is improvisational. By taking this approach, we feel agency in the process and we hone our problem-solving muscles.

The Difference between Ideology and Ideas

There's an obstacle to making an easier problem: ideology. You might be thinking, "What in the world does ideology have to do with solving for *x* or dividing fractions?" As you're about to discover, ideology can be an enabler of a fixed mindset, one that limits your options in math and life. Bear with me as I explain, and trust that I will return to math shortly.

Though I am no expert on politics, the national dialogue has obviously shifted in this decade with so many hot-button issues and constant outrage. As a result, I can see a change in my daily interactions. In many of my everyday conversations, ideology has replaced ideas. Ideologies make me nervous.

An ideology is a full belief system, a wide aperture lens through which you interpret most of the world. An idea is a specific concept, concrete or abstract. An ideological perspective might be to see everything through the lens of corporate greed or the lens of an overbearing government. Our social media–scrolling attention spans both simplify and amplify ideologies, making them more dangerous. They help us avoid wrestling with complex or confusing ideas. You can jump to your first answer, and the algorithm enables you to agree unthinkingly with yourself. You never have to bring the problem back up to consider. Ideologies are also efficient and necessary; they save us time. In our busy world, saturated with choices, we want and need shortcuts. An ideology about healthy food might help you eat better, even if your science is not accurate. We couldn't possibly think deeply about every issue that is thrown at us.

Ideological thinking, however, interferes with math teaching and learning. When I began to explore how to teach problem-solving, I found that ideology got in the way.

If we are ideological about math being about procedures, we look at the problem 35 × 18, solve it with the algorithm, and move on. We know the algorithm; in fact, many who wage the math wars are ideologically attached to using the algorithm irrespective of context. (Yes, in the world of math, a world you'd presume of cold logic, people become ideological about procedures; I was also astonished by this.) Others are ideologically opposed to the algorithm, which is even more confusing, considering its utility. The underlying thinking is that by learning the algorithm, you can't also learn to think creatively to solve math problems in another way.

Don't confuse making an easier problem with making a simplistic problem. It means you have to think for yourself, to move from ideology to ideas. Ideas are specific. They are discrete. Solving 35 × 18 with an algorithm is one idea. Solving it by rounding up 18 to 20 groups of 35 and then subtracting 2 groups of 35 is another idea. The technical math name of that idea is *compensation strategy*. Attempting to break 18 into a 10 and an 8 and attempting to multiply both numbers by 35 in your head and add them together is the *distributive property*. That is another idea.

Making an easier problem exists only in the realm of ideas. Ideas are harder work than ideologies because you have to think about the specifics; you have to think about each and every idea. On the other hand, the realm of ideas is inclusive. Everyone is encouraged to grapple with concepts, to question and analyze them. Everyone can have an idea on how to solve a problem, or at least a way to test it that may not succeed but still provides learning opportunities from the failed path. As Thomas Edison said, "I just found 2,000 ways not to make a lightbulb." Ideologies are exclusive. While they help us to form tribes—a purposeful endeavor in certain circumstances—they banish people who don't subscribe to a given ideology. The purpose of this whole book is to share many specific ideas on math teaching and learning in the hope I can explode the ideology around who is and isn't supposed to succeed at math.

Once we move from ideology to ideas, we are problem-solving, and we are born to solve problems. Other than the general good feeling that it creates in the brain, we can find genuine passion and purpose for the big and small problems with which we are grappling. For example, if we have been pursuing the perfect banana bread recipe, as we progress in the pursuit, our interest in hearing ideas for the best banana bread increases. I recently learned that if you put the nuts on a pan in the cold oven at the beginning, they'll be toasted the right amount when the oven beeps to signal it's done preheating. The more time I spend on specific ideas to solve a problem, the more passionate I become about it. I have come to love the specific problem of 35 × 18, similar to my pursuit of the perfect banana bread. I love to hear new solutions.

So let's return to 35 × 18. Here's one idea about how to solve the problem that has stayed with me because of how vividly this fifth grader described the picture in his head and his general enthusiasm for his strategy. He began by saying, "In math, one thing I *love* is area, so I think of this as a rectangle and calculate the area. I break it up into smaller rectangles and add them up."

Me: "Wow, that's wonderful. Tell me more about why you love area."

Him: "Because area shows me that math is real. Area is the amount of space on the floor of my bedroom. Area makes sense to me."

Here's what I envisioned as he was speaking.

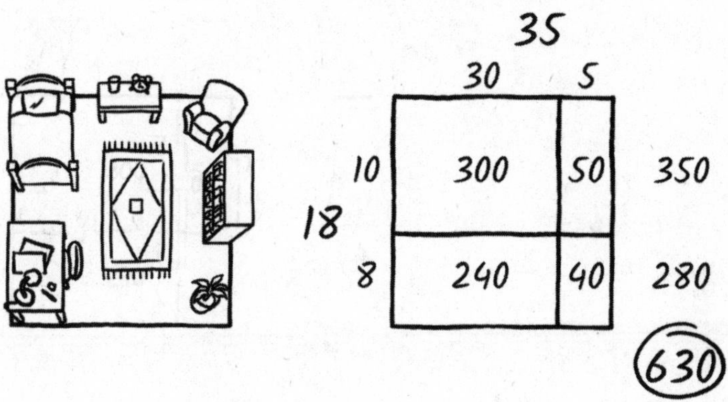

"I calculate each rectangle and add them up—300, 50, 240, and 40." He paused for a minute. "I think that is 630, but I might have done that part wrong in my head."

A couple years into sharing this problem with kids and adults, I met an educator, Denise, who shared a new, easier way. Her way sent a jolt of delight through my body when I heard it. This problem-solving idea for 35 × 18 has become my favorite and the way I try to solve similar problems.

Denise is a processor; she likes to think before speaking. I had discussed the problem with her in the afternoon. She listened, but offered no immediate solutions. She said she wanted to turn it over in her mind and get back to me. Later that evening she sent me a brief note that went something like this:

I was thinking
about the problem
and thought of
an easier way
35x18 = 70x9
70x9 = 630

Mind blown. Denise had realized that 35 × 18 had a 2 in the 18 that she could move over to the 35 to make 70.

$$35 \times 18 = 35 \times (2 \times 9) = (35 \times 2) \times 9 = 70 \times 9$$

The technical name for this strategy is the *associative property*. The associative property means we can multiply 35 × 2 × 9 in any order and still get the same number, 630. The name of this strategy doesn't matter, but the axiom does. Making an easier problem requires us to engage with specific ideas. When we engage at this level, we have a chance to explore the rules of numbers more deeply. These are the rules to which there are no exceptions—the pure axioms. Math students who make easier problems come to know the axioms of mathematics intuitively through play.

In the classic book *Zen and the Art of Motorcycle Maintenance* the narrator criticizes a motorcycle maintenance manual making a similar point: "What's really angering about instructions of this sort is that they imply there's only one way to put a rotisserie together—their way. And that presumption wipes out creativity. Actually, there are hundreds of ways to put the rotisserie together and when they make you follow just one way without showing you the overall problem the instructions become hard to follow in such a way as not to make mistakes. You lose feeling for the work. And not only that, it's very unlikely that they've told you the best way."

I sometimes forget how much courage it takes to ask for help, until I need help once again. I pride myself on my self-sufficiency, which makes it even harder to ask. Students who discover that trying another way is a normal part of problem-solving learn to ask for help. They may say, "Could you show me another way?" Or "I didn't understand your question; could you ask me a different way?"

Help-seeking behavior is highly predictive of academic success. Asking for clarification and receiving feedback from a teacher or friend can make a problem easier—much easier. In school, help-seeking behavior can look like many things: asking for advice, requesting assistance with a task, or asking a specific question about something you don't understand.

While many factors influence a person's willingness to engage in help-seeking behavior, learning science advocates a feedback-rich environment to facilitate it. Over the last decade, I have visited thousands of elementary math classes. Many will have anchor charts around the room. One I see so often is "Making mistakes is how you learn." That is the best "slogan" of a feedback-rich environment. But kids know that those posters are often a lie. Children are not dumb. They know school and math classes are high stakes. And making mistakes results in punishment.

Watch those same kids play video games. When they fail a quest or a battle, they seek help, they try again. They parse their problem. They are certainly engaged in ideas, not ideology. In play, they look to make their problems easier. Video games aren't trying to discourage players from playing to winnow down the population to the real Video Game Kids. In that space, kids understand that failing is the first step to success.

I love to catch middle school math teachers in a reflective moment. Middle school teachers are made of special stuff. When they reflect on the differences between their students who succeed and those who struggle, they rarely find the primary difference was innate intelligence. Instead, these teachers often describe help-seeking behavior as the differentiator. Here are a few responses I've gotten:

"My stronger students sought help to understand, and they

used their time well. They parsed the problem, and focused their questions on the specific part that confused them."

"I reflect on middle school kids solving complex, multistep word problems. Many of these problems would be five or six steps. Nearly all my students would get the most sophisticated math work correct. But some would take a cumbersome step to solve a calculation and make a careless mistake. It was heartbreaking because the kids who were getting it right were actually solving an easier problem, and the kids getting it wrong were creating a very complex problem in the middle of an even more complex problem. When I finally realized this, I began to shift my teaching to intentionally help all my students make easier problems."

Experienced teachers notice the subtle problem-solving habits and mindsets of their students and, in addition to teaching the concepts and procedures, want to build these muscles.

Ultimately, we are talking about more than help seeking; we are talking about your problem-solving preferences or your problem-solving style.

Think back to the myths we've discussed. Does speeding through math help you pause to make an easier problem? Yes and no. Under stress, the blood leaves the brain and moves to the legs so you can run. That's not a formula for the cognitive pause required to try an easier way. However, without the working memory, you run out of steam for the interesting parts of the problem. As I've shared, making an easier problem is not a trick to be memorized; it is accomplished through a collaborative discussion. You absolutely can't memorize your way to making an easier problem. But, memorizing algorithms and processes is a great help, and frankly necessary knowledge, to this collaboration. And finally, if you are told to follow someone else's exact way, that's the formula to stifle your courage and intuition so that you are certain not to know that you are allowed to make an easier problem. Making an easier problem is about developing your own problem-solving style, and it's a virtuous cycle. When you find an easier way for you, it makes you more confident. When you are confident, you are more likely to explore to make an easier problem.

CHAPTER 8

Try a Different Way

LET'S SAY I AM TRYING TO DESCALE MY COFFEE MA-chine. I am pressing buttons and heading down a specific path. If it doesn't work, what should I do? Yell at the machine? It has happened. Wish I had a degree in industrial engineering? Not something I can complete before I want to make my next coffee. But at some point, reason will give way, and I will do the only rational thing I can do. I will try another way. Clicking many buttons. Finding a tutorial on YouTube. Asking a family member for help.

Trying another way can be a scrappy or even a desperate approach. It can also be a calm and orderly response, if you're aware that part of problem-solving involves stepping away or changing the context.

While it's expected in the domain of home improvement, many people unfortunately don't realize that "trying another way" is a critical part of math, too. I didn't fully internalize this strategy until my late thirties. Those who know it save a lot of energy and emotion and can get on with problem-solving. This includes three-year-olds playing a stacking or counting game or me making coffee. This is a math skill and a life skill, and we should teach it as soon as kids are able to absorb it.

Even without this skill, when we get frustrated, we eventually cool off and, hopefully, come back to the problem and try another way. However, we don't have metacognition of what we are doing. That is, we aren't contemplating our mental processes or thinking about how we are thinking. We don't understand that having to try a different way is normal. And, hopefully, knowing it's normal brings more people back into problem-solving rather than their giving up on the math problem in front of them or even learning math itself.

Math learning often does not unfold this way. Typically, if you get stuck or stumble, it's viewed negatively. You may be given a battery of stigmatizing tests and then dubiously classified as "two grade levels behind," whatever that means. Having been classified, you are most certainly pulled off the problems you were initially working with and enter a remedial track. You do not get to try the problem in a new way.

While math instruction's essence is problem-solving (and often represents the only time K–12 students are actually problem-solving in the school day) trying a different way is not sufficiently embedded in math teaching and learning. We have somehow forgotten its value for real life when we move into the classroom environment.

Trying a Different Way by Design

When my family travels, we play games—card or board games and more recently all the games available on the Play section of the *New York Times* digital edition. One game we love in the *Times* app is called Spelling Bee. In the game, you are given seven letters, laid out in a six-sided array around one letter in the center, and you have to use them to make as many words of four or more letters as you can, always including the middle letter. A word that uses all the letters is called a pangram, which results in screams of joy in our family.

I was introduced to Spelling Bee by one of my sons, who had been playing the game for a few weeks. That day's puzzle featured letters *R, M, F, U, A, L,* and *O,* with *O* the middle letter. We were rattling off words together: *loaf, loom, from, room, aloof.* But then we hit a block. Neither of us could think of another word.

My son looked at me and said, "Let me help you, Mama," and he pressed a little button at the bottom of the screen. The six letters around the *O* changed places. It was the same set of letters, the same game, the same constraints. But just moving the position of the letters made both of our brains kick back on. We looked at each other and shouted in unison, "*FORMULA!*"—the pangram.

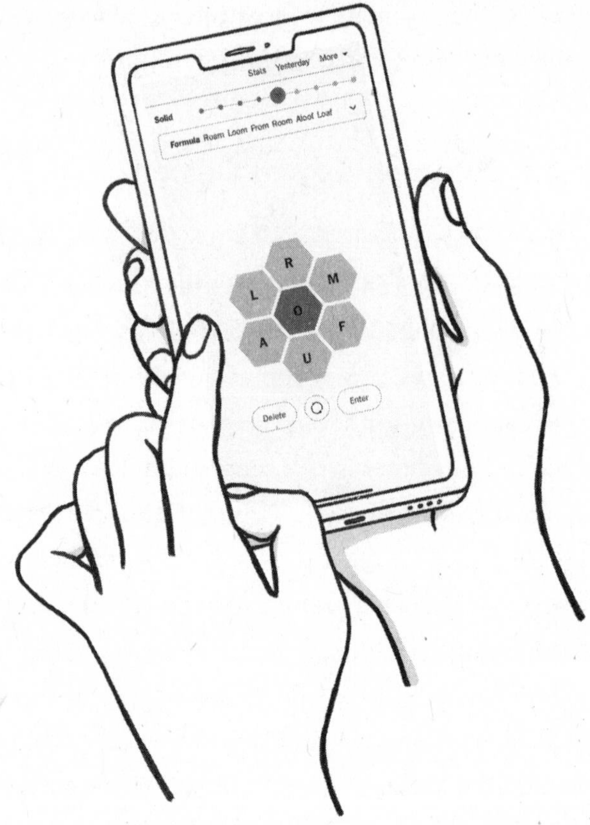

The game designers reveal an understanding of the mechanics of problem-solving and how to create an enjoyable experience, and thus anticipated that players would need to look at the game a new way when they got stuck. This design capitalizes on the problem-solving benefit of trying a different way. Note in Spelling Bee how subtle, calm, and expected trying another way can be.

That is, unfortunately, the opposite of how we generally approach math learning. The reason for this is a false metaphor for how math understanding is built. We say that math is cumulative—that each new concept depends on having mastered all the concepts that came before it. While it is true that math is cumulative, our discussion and interpretation of it resides at the logical extreme. The belief becomes that solving the problem in front of you requires rigidly applying each and every prerequisite skill. Or that each year we build up our understanding as a foundation, assuming that if we are missing bricks, the wall will crumble. If you can't do the math in front of you, it isn't because you have to try another way, it is because you have not filled each and every brick in the wall. In fact, trying a different way would be lunacy if you believe that every single brick has to be mortared in place first. This is far too literal an interpretation of how to build a mathematical mind. Math is only a few big ideas and there are many entry points. It is not hundreds of discrete skills—unless we are teaching the myths of math.

Let's say a third grader is struggling with fractions, or a sixth grader is struggling with ratios and rates, which are two consequential topics in math; we assume they are grade levels behind and spend our time filling the missing bricks in the foundation. In reality, there are no bricks to fill because sometimes math has fresh starts, or to extend the metaphor, there are new walls to build.

Every single thing in math is not cumulative. You could learn what a fraction is even if you're still memorizing your multiplication tables. You could be solidifying your understanding of ratios, taught in sixth grade, but be able to find the volume of a rectangular prism with ease in seventh. Sometimes when you struggle, you have nowhere to go back to. We don't teach fractions in first or second grade. So if you're a third grader struggling with fractions, you're grappling with a new idea—that there are numbers between 0 and 1 on the number line. We also don't teach ratios or proportional reasoning before sixth grade. So, if you struggle, there are really no remedial options. We have to try another way to present the same concept.

Because math is filled with fresh starts, we need to utilize a different approach when students are confused. If a sixth-grade student is asked to explain why 4:6 and 6:18 are not equivalent ratios, there is truly nowhere in the previous grades K–5 to look for remedial content. So here, we must try another way.

One approach might be to try to alter these ratios so that they have a number in common. Taking 4:6 and dividing a 2 from both sides would make it 2:3. Dividing a 3 out of both sides of 6:18 would make it 2:6. Through this abstract manipulation, we can see that both ratios are not equivalent. But the underlying process may not make sense at first to students.

Instead, we might try visualizing or concretizing these numbers (refer back to Chapter 6 for a refresher). Imagine you have 4 cans of black paint and 6 cans of white paint and you mix them together. Now imagine you have 6 cans of black paint and 18 cans of white paint and you mix them together. Will the mixtures be the same color gray? Which mixture will be a lighter color?

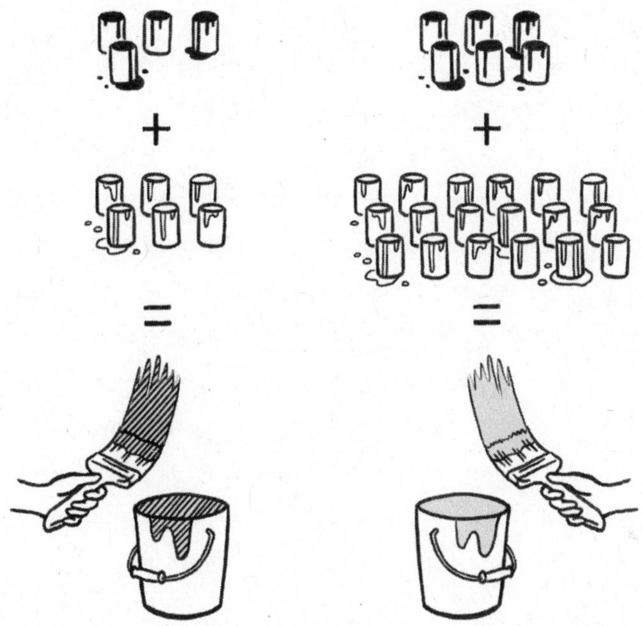

Another approach might be to make the problem more relevant to your life or to explain the math in the context of something you already understand. Perhaps I can't understand ratios abstractly, but I get them intuitively through my love of football. I am a football fan with unwavering loyalty to the Buffalo Bills (#BillsMafia). In my family, our loyalty runs deep and across generations. If someone tells me that the score of the football game is 45–0 and it is halftime, I would ask them to clarify. That score would give me pause. I know that halftime means we have two more quarters to go and it's not a normal thing to see the score so high in a game with only 2 quarters completed. NFL games don't typically reach a score of 90, so 2 quarters to 45 points might imply 4 quarters to 90 points. In other words, the ratio of touchdowns to quarters played *feels* off. Because the game has relevance, I'm aware that the ratio is unusual in football, even if I can't pinpoint that ratio with a formula.

Research on relevance in the fields of teaching and learning reading are applicable to math in certain ways. Here's what the famed cognitive scientist Daniel Willingham summarized in a piece in *The New York Times*:

> *In one experiment, third graders—some identified by a reading test as good readers, some as poor—were asked to read a passage about soccer. The poor readers who knew a lot about soccer were three times as likely to make accurate inferences about the passage as the good readers who didn't know much about the game. That implies that students who score well on reading tests are those with broad knowledge; they usually know at least a little about the topics of the passages on the test.*

In math, helping students with relevant word problem contexts instead of nonsensical ones is a way to tap into their intuition and previous knowledge and try another way. I have seen word problems and wondered, "Why would I buy thirty cantaloupes?"

Relevance as a strategy, of course, has its limits. Jerome Bruner, one of the scientists who synthesized the concrete to pictorial to abstract teaching approach, wrote, "It is sentimentalism to assume that the teaching of life can always be fitted to the child's interests, just as it is empty formalism to force the child to parrot the formulas of adult society. Interests can be created and stimulated." Said another way, my seventh-grade twin boys simply cannot read only about dragons and do math problems that involve WWII artillery.

Helping math students discover another approach that works for them is sometimes technical and requires quite a bit of knowledge on how to teach math, otherwise known as pedagogical content knowledge. A common approach in math classrooms might drop a fourth-grade student who struggles with an element of fourth-grade math to a lower grade level. But while the intention is to help, it often wastes time.

Consider the following:

$$\begin{array}{r} 4072 \\ -2429 \\ \hline \end{array}$$

This is a fourth-grade subtraction problem that asks us to "regroup," or break up one 1,000 to make ten 100s. (Colloquially, we often call this "borrowing.") Fourth graders might struggle here, particularly with the 0 in the hundreds place. If a student answers the question incorrectly, however, instead of addressing the confusion over the 0, a common practice might be to drop the student back to a second-grade problem when multi-digit subtraction was first introduced. In that case, the student would next see a problem like this:

$$21 - 13 =$$

But second graders may use a less-developed strategy than the full subtraction algorithm to solve this problem. While they could borrow a 1 from the 2 in the tens column of 21, the problem also lends itself to a simpler counting strategy, which might sound like this if verbalized: *I know that 13 needs 7 to get to 20. One more makes 21. Seven and 1 are 8!* Said another way, moving a fourth grader who is struggling with the advanced strategy of regrouping or borrowing to a problem that doesn't require the use of that strategy is nothing more than wasting his time. It does not help a fourth grader get any closer to understanding the concept of regrouping in the subtraction algorithm or what to do with the 0 than he originally stumbled on.

Here's how our example student, if struggling, might access this fourth-grade problem if we tried to present the same subtraction problem another way instead. We could draw a place value chart and turn each number into a picture that shows how many thousands, hundreds, tens, and ones are in it. Then we could show how 1,000 can become 10 hundreds, how a 10 can become 10 ones, in addition to how the subtraction is happening. This is a math picture of the problem 4,072 – 2,429:

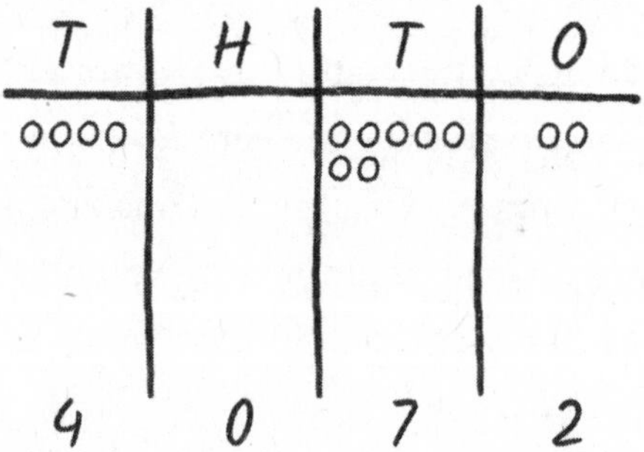

T	H	T	O
oooo		ooooo oo	oo
4	0	7	2

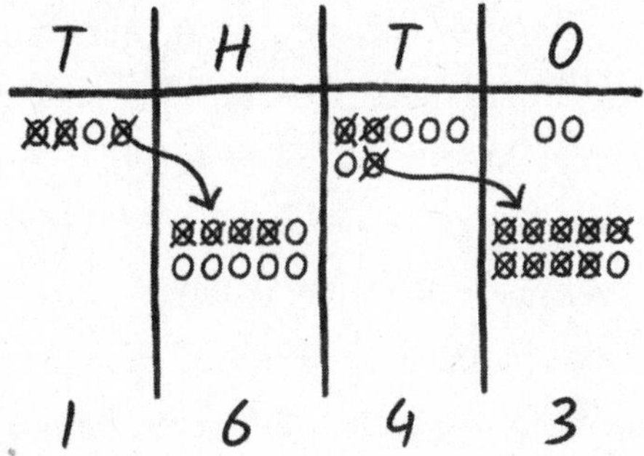

Using a visual representation, we can stay with the same problem and try a different way. We can also key in to the big idea the fourth-grade student is still shaky on—how to regroup.

Catching Up and Moving Forward

In the early years of building Zearn—before we had much data, or the data scientists on our team to work with them—we stepped back to conduct a rudimentary analysis of our digital learning approach. The key question we wanted to answer was: What helped students get a question right when they had gotten a similar question wrong initially? In addition, we wanted to help students as fast as possible. Time is the scarcest resource in learning.

We found something unexpected. When students who had gotten something wrong were then shown another way of solving the problem, one involving simple pictures often with bright colors, they were more likely to get a similar problem correct the next time they encountered it. We didn't really know what to make of this finding. We surmised the pictures made the concept accessible, and the bright colors grabbed students' attention.

A few years ago, with research and data scientists on board as well as more than fourteen billion completed problems in our dataset, we returned to this line of inquiry. During the depths of the pandemic, I was talking to Steve Levitt, of *Freakonomics* fame. He asked what we send students back to work on when they struggle, and I explained that in math, there is often nowhere to go back to. The answer, I added, isn't always to revert to a lower grade level but to show students another way that's appropriate for their current level.

The dominant schema, I told him, is often a waste of kids' time. Sometimes students do need to go back and review earlier material (once again, integrative complexity), but the reflex to send them back immediately, no matter what, is misguided.

Levitt challenged my team: If what we were saying was true, we should prove it. He assured us that our dataset was sufficiently robust. He also shared creative ideas on how to find a natural experiment in our dataset.

Our researchers got to work. Eventually, we utilized cutting-edge data science methods. First, they built a "fixed effect" model. This is a model where the two comparison groups are not separate groups of people, as you might find in standard research, but the same people compared when they experience different stimuli at distinct moments in time.

Usually, when we run an experiment, we compare the impact of an intervention on two similar groups. If we are going to determine if a medicine works, we give the medicine to one group and a placebo (like a sugar pill) to the other. But rather than comparing one cohort of students to another cohort of students, our researchers compared students against themselves. They broke down the times in the Zearn app when the same students were left on grade level to be shown another approach to a problem, compared to times when the same students were taken off grade level and put on a remediation track.

For those of you who spend time with kids as educators, parents, or caregivers, you know that kids can behave in strikingly distinct ways based on the stimuli they are exposed to. In this model design, we saw what happened to the exact same kids when they were able to stay on grade level and shown a different way, compared to when they were taken off grade level and remediated in the traditional way.

Even though we were responding to Levitt's challenge and trying to prove what we already believed was happening, we were still shocked by the strength of the findings. People use the expression "fall out of my chair." And I never knew what that meant until I saw the findings of our analysis and fell out of my chair. It was a rolling chair;

I had my elbows on the desk and my head cupped in my hands. As I was reading the first draft, I was so shocked that my body jerked. The chair rolled back. Boom! I hit the floor and bumped my head on the desk on the way down. Here's what caused me to tumble: When the same student was shown a different way, she struggled less than when she was taken back and remediated with previous grade-level content. And of course, because these students stayed on grade level, they completed more grade-level content.

Remember, students were being taken off grade level to make math less a struggle for them, but the opposite phenomenon was occurring. They were struggling more! That is completely counterintuitive. Based on the research we have done to date, we can only guess at the reason. Maybe they got discouraged, felt stigmatized. Maybe they had still been puzzling over the math in front of them and now were doing some other math altogether and that was confusing. Perhaps telling them they weren't advanced enough for the problems they were struggling with became a self-fulfilling prophecy.

Imagine a seventh-grade student is learning negative numbers and while learning about those (for the first time), she encounters decimal operations, which she is fuzzy on because she learned those during the pandemic-disrupted years of schooling. In the context of an engaging lesson to make sense of negative numbers where we are descending a mountain (positive numbers), passing sea level (0), and then diving into the ocean (negative numbers), she sees a problem, 1.4 ÷ 2, and she is stuck. She doesn't know what to do. A remediation approach would take her back to weeks of fourth- and fifth-grade work to build up her knowledge of decimals. She might be practicing naming the tenths, hundredths, and thousandths place or doing pages of decimal division worksheets for weeks. She would completely stop progress on learning negative numbers during this time.

Now let's consider a different way.

When she struggled with 1.4 ÷ 2, we could show her this problem next. What is 14 ÷ 2? 7. Right. Easy. Then we could say, decimal operations are exactly like whole numbers operations, so you are very close to understanding this question. At this moment, many students wouldn't need more of a prompt and would say 0.7. Others may need a bit more instruction on how the decimal point works, what it means, and a reminder that all the rules of base 10 apply whether we are working with whole numbers or decimals. The alternative way doesn't have to be anything complex—just a nudge toward an alternative attempt can allow kids to leapfrog forward.

Sleep on It

Going to sleep may not seem like an active try, but it can help you feel refreshed and eager to start on the problem anew. Or leaving the problem for a while, doing something else in the interim. The subconscious mind will keep working. Once in college, I was working through a philosophy paper and I had thoroughly confused myself. The paper was about the debate between pre-Socratic early Greek philosophers on whether the universe was composed of elements or atoms and the void. My task was to pick a philosopher, dissect his arguments, and prove him wrong. In tears, I went to bed. It was freshman year and impostor syndrome overwhelmed me. I was certain I would fail, and I would have to call my parents, tell them I was a disappointment, and drop out. I woke up earlier than my class, somewhat miraculously. Even more remarkable, I woke up with the answer. It had all clicked. The way to disprove the pre-Socratic philosopher's assertions that I had read was to point out that infinity was not the same as eternity. The pre-Socratic philosopher had used them interchangeably and thus tricked me into believing they were the same. That trick was key to his argument. In the night my brain was able to untie that knot. I went to my Apple IIc and banged out the answer. Infinity is space and time, and eternity is only time. Many luminaries have been known to keep a pen and pad of paper next to them at night so they can jot down their middle-of-the-night brainstorms (when I tried this, the results were not brilliant; your mileage may vary).

When I talk to people about the idea of pressing ahead by trying a different way rather than going backward, I tend to notice a three-step reaction. Step 1: Huh? I don't understand what you are saying. If I can talk them through, as we've just done, we get to Step 2: The shoulders drop and the face relaxes. I think that is because deep down, we all know that intuition is key; we don't have to quash it to succeed in problem-solving. Said another way, problem-solving is what we are all naturally good at. And then finally, I am happiest when I get to the final step. Step 3: A smile. Yep, problem-solving is fun, but only if we all remember that we will need to sometimes try doing it another way. And that trying a different way is, in fact, part of the fun itself.

CHAPTER 9

Practice with Purpose

NEARLY A DECADE AGO, I HEARD THIS BIT OF WISDOM from a little boy:

"There is no such thing as smart, only hard work."

When the parent of this wise child joined Zearn to lead our approach to teaching and learning, she told me that *genius* is a bad word when I kept saying it. She's right. While we celebrate hard work in other fields, in STEM, the primary narrative is still of the lone genius, not of a team or an individual who worked hard. In fact, the cult of genius is so overemphasized in STEM that hard work is often considered something to be ashamed of—if the answers don't come easily and naturally, it's a sign you don't belong there at all.

This narrative didn't arise entirely by accident or misunderstanding. Some cultivate it. They may intentionally leave their books at school in a visible spot, instead of taking them home to study, to make other students believe their success is effortless. In truth, they have a second copy of the book at home. One story in particular changed my thinking about the whole lone genius mystique altogether. Michelangelo, the most celebrated Renaissance artist, who painted the Sistine Chapel and sculpted David, jealously guarded his sketches, never selling them or allowing them to circulate. As he sensed his death was approaching, he burned every sketch in his studio in Rome in two giant bonfires, and thus few survive. Giorgi Vasari, a biographer of Renaissance artists, postulates that Michelangelo did this to maintain an aura of perfection.

This kind of cultivated narrative may help us excuse our failures in science or math: If we're not doing well, it's because we're not inherently exceptional. Or more likely, we don't reflect deeply on the myth of lone genius and just accept it because it's repeated so often and everywhere we go. But we pay a price for this acceptance. It dissuades students from pursuing careers in science, technology, engineering, and math. It contributes to the leaky STEM pipeline—in which 30 to 50 percent of students who declare a STEM major at the outset of college change majors to a non-STEM field within three years. These numbers are significantly higher for women and Black and Latino students. Many become discouraged because they believe that genius, rather than hard work, is the only way to become a successful scientist.

The truth is that math achievement, like success in any endeavor, depends on hard work. But not just any kind of hard work. What math requires is *practice with purpose.* Done right, this kind of practice can help people not only become better at math but derive more enjoyment from doing it.

Spreading the Word

To encourage practicing with purpose, which I will define shortly, we need to tell stories illustrating the value of this practice. These are stories with the following moral: Practice is required. One study conducted by Penn State University researchers found that telling the stories of success in STEM forged through hard work, struggle, and practice, as opposed to attributing it to some type of genetic anomaly like being a genius, motivated young people to stay in those fields. As one of the researchers put it, "The combined results suggest that when you assume that someone's success is linked to effort, that is more motivating than hearing about a genius's predestined success story."

The researchers shared, for example, stories of Thomas Edison failing over and over, as well as tales of unnamed scientists (actually made-up characters) muddling through, which were contrasted to the genius of Albert Einstein. The young people considering STEM fields were more motivated by the stories of concerted effort. Hard work, or practicing, can be drudgery and a waste of time, or it can be productive and satisfying. It can even be fun. In fields without as many myths and anxiety surrounding achievement, practicing is not laden with so much baggage. We have many starting thoughts about math practice to contend with. But, as in all fields, to succeed in math, we have to practice.

You can learn some things in a few days or weeks of focused effort—French braiding hair or jumping rope (two skills on my personal mastery wish list). Other skills take months or years to learn, like being fluent in another language or becoming literate or numerate. Whether the new learning is on the simpler or more complex side, it requires practice, and the right kind of practice is both necessary to and can speed up the process. Psychologist Anders Ericsson calls it deliberate practice.

In his book *Peak*, Ericsson defines deliberate practice as an effortful and intentional activity designed to improve performance. It has five elements: setting specific and challenging goals, focused attention, immediate feedback, repetition, and gradual improvement. In his research, he studied individuals who have achieved seemingly impossible feats, such as having a superhuman memory or becoming a world-class musician. As Malcolm Gladwell famously noted, about 10,000 hours of practice is required to achieve expertise, and Ericsson's research was his source.

Studies also bridge the work of practice from world-class performance to teaching and learning anything. Cognitive scientist Daniel Willingham, who translates the latest brain science into ideas that teachers and students can use in their daily practice, has relevant insight here. As he says,

"Memory is the residue of thought." (The phrase comes up frequently around my office when we're building new math lessons.) Willingham asks us to consider why we often forget what we came to fetch in the kitchen but can remember a marketing jingle from years ago. "To teach well," he says, "you should pay careful attention to what an assignment will actually make students think about (not what you hope they will think about), because that is what they will remember."

When I first read this passage, I flashed back to second grade. The day in question has always been a puzzle for me. Our teacher gave each of us a small, cleaned baby-food container, then filled them with some heavy cream. We screwed on the lids ourselves, and she tightened them. She then told us to shake the jars as hard as we could. She turned on dance music to help us move.

I remember all my classmates jumping up and down, running about the room, and vigorously shaking those jars. Every time we'd be ready to stop, the teacher encouraged us to keep going. The task seemed to go on forever; my arm hurt from all the shaking. At the end, when the lids came off, we each had something in our baby-food jar vaguely resembling churned butter. I was certain of one thing. I was not going to eat what was in there.

What I have never figured out is why we did it at all. I have tried many times to reconstruct what the lesson was supposed to be about. Sometimes I tell myself it must have been about how the Pilgrims and Native Americans churned butter for Thanksgiving. Other times, I think it must have been a science class about states of matter. Finally, I wonder if we were just making butter to make butter. It left me with a lifelong memory—and the knowledge that churning butter by shaking a jar is extremely hard to do, especially when you're seven—but whatever it was that the teacher hoped to teach us, I never learned.

There is a great deal of "churning butter" in math practice as well. Math learning is often filled with long worksheets with unrelated problems that provide no opportunity for immediate feedback. In the digital realm where feedback is usually immediate, I have seen countless math-practice games with complex game mechanics that focus the learner more on how to score the points (such as the precision required to shoot the duck or the dexterity needed to feed the fish) than the math. I have seen other activities that have interstitial moments that are long and simply baffling; I still think only about those and don't remember the math myself. I have seen practice websites featuring animated characters scratching their rear ends or washing dishes while unrelated sounds play, like maracas shaking. I have no idea why.

You might think, "So what, it's a game." But if the "fun" part of practice moves to the forefront, it will distract learners from the specific thing they're practicing. Further, it's taxing for the mind and harms learning to practice the wrong thing. The worst of these games award points for randomly guessing, meaning getting the mathematics wrong! Having to unlearn the wrong math is worse than never having learned it at all.

Consider how hard it is to unlearn something. Somehow, I never mastered the difference between the words *lose* and *loose*, so I mix them up all the time. Similarly, one of my twin sons got east and west consistently mixed up in his mind. We live in New York City, which he believed to be the West Coast. When we spoke about the West Coast or pointed west to show where the sun set or pointed east to show him the Atlantic Ocean, he would be confused. He made it through this mental bug and now knows that the Pacific Ocean is west of the United States. But because memory is the residue of thought, he had to unlearn that the Atlantic Ocean was to the west of New York, and then relearn that it was to the east. This is a heavy mental burden.

In my observations in classrooms and in digital tools, I notice two primary reasons for wasteful practice. The first is "churning butter": The learning activity has too much of my attention devoted to something that is not what I am supposed to learn. The second reason is that the practice is overwhelming. Athletes, whether elite ones or Little Leaguers, don't get better by playing an entire game over and over. Musicians don't progress by playing a piece end to end repeatedly. Instead, they focus on the discrete chunks of the task they need to improve to make progress.

This is why the best chess players work on openings and end games slavishly, rather than muddling through the indecisive middle sections. A key to practice is finding the right chunks that support progress.

In music, it is common for novices or students who progress more slowly to speed through the easy parts and stumble through the harder parts of a piece. Musicians who progress more quickly in learning a new work, and in improving their musical capacity overall, do things differently. When they first encounter a composition, they identify the difficult part, and master that early by practicing that section far more. This smooths out the piece when they practice all the way through.

And it's not just the hard parts that they break into chunks. Musicians who are deliberate about practice divide up the whole piece and learn it in sections. If they simply played everything through, it would overwhelm their brains and keep them from learning efficiently. And by practicing the whole composition through before mastering the hard parts, you might incorporate mistakes into your practice, until you have to unlearn them—like unlearning that the Atlantic Ocean is west of New York—thereby increasing the time it will take you to master the piece the right way.

Math requires the same chunking, the same discrete practice. It may sound dull to repeat the same few bars of music over and over again. But making practice discrete enough to be helpful doesn't mean it becomes rote and boring.

Think about a worksheet with problems like these . . .

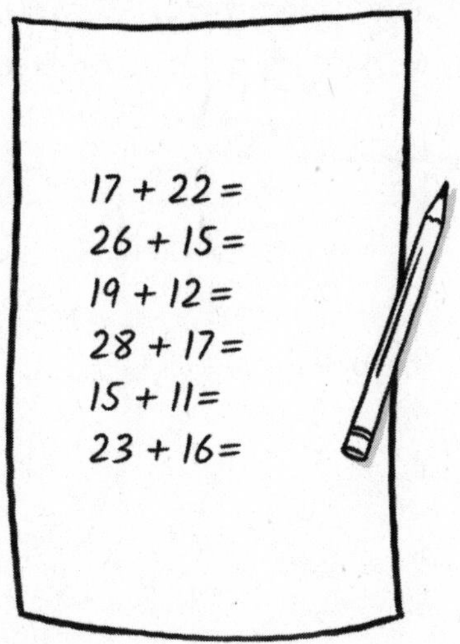

Here are the answers filled in.

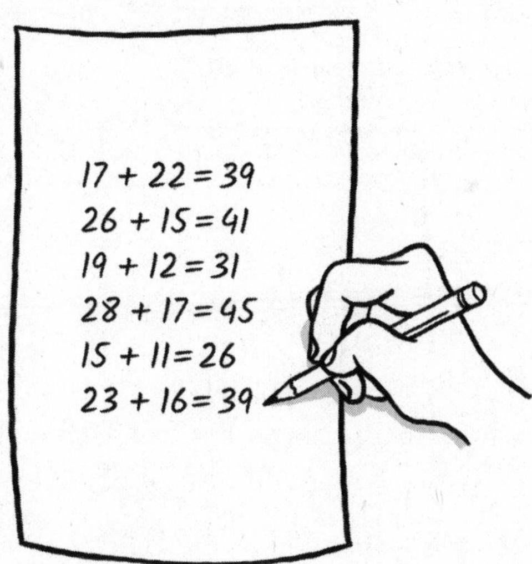

Can you see any purpose or system here? What would you learn by completing this worksheet? You'd be doing some two-digit addition problems that sometimes made you regroup in the ones place. The only goal is to practice addition.

Now consider worksheets made of problem sequences like this:

17 + 13 =
17 + 14 =
16 + 14 =
16 + 15 =
15 + 15 =
15 + 16 =

Here are the problems filled in.

Or this:

35 + 25 =
25 + 35 =
60 - 25 =
60 - 35 =
43 + 17 =
17 + 43 =
60 - 43 =
60 - 17 =

Again, here are the problems filled in.

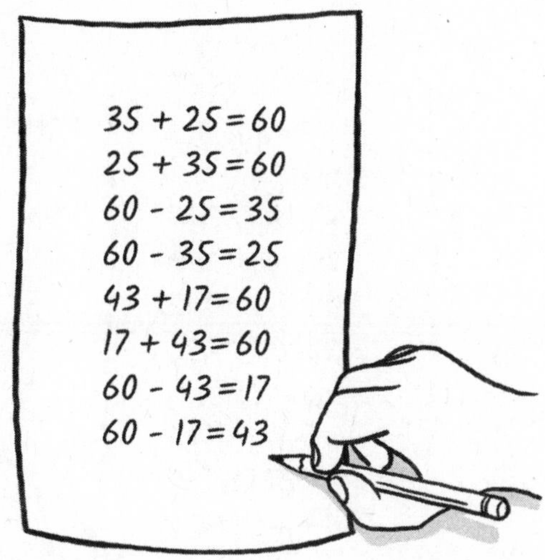

Here's a final set.

3 x 2 =
3 x 20 =
3 x 200 =
3 x 2000 =
2000 x 3 =
3 x 5=
3 x 50=
3 x 500=
3 x 5000=
5000 x 3=

And here are the answers.

How would you articulate the purpose of these practice sets in contrast? For the first set, the purpose might be to prime your brain with ten pairs, 3 and 7, 4 and 6, 5 and 5, in preparation for the harder addition problem that follows. It might reveal a strategy—when you see 17 + 14, you can turn that into 17 + 13 + 1 in your mind. You might also contemplate how many ways there are to make 30 and 31. You might even smile upon discovering a pattern—the answer will always be either 30 or 31. And as you do all these things, you also practice addition.

In the second set, the purpose could be to remind the learner that math is autodidactic, meaning you can check your work to make sure you are right, and figuring out whether you're right or wrong doesn't depend on anybody else's judgment or authority. When adults and children describe their love of math, many will mention how empowering this quality is. I have watched children do this exact set and answer incorrectly for 35 + 25, but when they see 60 – 25, they jump back and correct the first two problems. So here children are practicing addition and subtraction, *and* they are learning the relationship between them. By seeing the relationships among the problems and answers, they are automatically practicing the "check your work" strategy that math inherently offers.

In the final set, children are practicing multiplication and playing with 0s or, as we call it in mathematics, *place value*. Looking at the products, we are seeing the zeros grow as we multiply 3 by bigger and bigger numbers. Children (and adults) need to spend time with zeros to appreciate the scale difference between these numbers. And the final question in the 3 × 2 and 3 × 5 sequence asks the learner to remember what happens when we flip the numbers. Nothing! 3 × 2,000 = 2,000 × 3. This is called the *commutative property*, but rather than talk about it or learn how to spell it, it's most fun to play with it when practicing.

The world is full of patterns and structures, and humans love finding patterns and structure—in art, architecture, and music. We love patterns the way we love the taste of something sweet; it's our nature. By bringing out patterns, these practice sets accomplish more and are more engaging for everyone. It's like solving a mystery. It pleases us; to my claim at the outset of this book, it calms our soul. It is a thing of beauty. We can bring this beauty to math practice itself, allowing it to have a higher purpose and inspiring kids to do it. Because we can't rewire the brain and create a numerate mind without practice.

If we are spending time practicing math (or really doing anything), we should use that time well. Think about the five practice sets above. Even if you don't feel particularly soothed or drawn into enjoying the patterns, the bottom three simply get more learning done per problem. In a crowded world where time is at a premium, our practice problems must achieve many learning objectives. Math, like everything, requires practice. We can either practice with purpose and get more out of it or we can make it drudgery.

Language Practice

We've discussed how building a math problem-solving mind, from pre-K to algebra, is similar to language learning. This extends to how we practice. We build language automaticity with practice, until it's something we do without thinking about it. Let's say you learn a new vocabulary word: *gumption*. Gumption is a mix of courage and initiative. You hear the word all the time, you practice using the word in your head, and soon, you will be able to use it in a sentence without even consciously trying to do so. It will just escape your lips as you are talking, and you will realize you have used the word after you have said it.

The same thing happens in math. We have considerable evidence from many studies, as well as from the Zearn dataset, that it is easier for young children to add than subtract. If you ask a small child, "What is 6 plus 2?" "8!" She'll take less time coming up with the answer than she will if you ask her, "What is 7 minus 3?" ". . . 4?" Further, her answer to the subtraction question may not be as certain. Why is that? Why is subtraction so much harder than addition?

The answer is that we practice counting forward with children significantly more than we practice counting backward. If you have ever had surgery, your anesthesiologist may have asked you to count backward from 100. They do this because it takes concentration to count backward, producing two benefits. First, it takes your mind off your anxieties about the procedure. Second, it allows the anesthesiologist to monitor how quickly the medicine is working. Counting backward from 100 is effortful, whereas counting forward to 100 is effortless. That is simply because of practice—or the lack thereof.

When children first start adding and subtracting, one of the early strategies they use is to "count on": To add 2 to 6, they'll start at 6 and then count in their heads or on their fingers to get two more, saying 6, 7(1), 8(2). They can recall instantly that 7 and 8 come after 6. But when they subtract or go in the other direction, they don't have instant recall: 7, 6(1), 5(2), 4(3). A wonderful way to build a young child's skill, capacity, and enjoyment of addition and subtraction is to practice counting forward and backward starting from any number. For example, when counting, we should vary it: 1, 2, 3, 4, 5, but also 17, 16, 15, 14 . . .

Consider the use of uppercase versus lowercase letters. In many preschools, or homes with young children, you will see posters featuring uppercase letters on the walls. However, in this book and any writing, the vast majority of letters are lowercase. For years, I kept a note taped to my desk that my first-grade teacher made for me with *b, d, p,* and *q* demystified. These subtle decisions to never count backward or to rarely show young children lowercase letters to practice have a cost.

Every year I do this work offers more evidence that all kids are math kids. Each year millions of students complete billions of problems on our web application—to date, fourteen billion. When we analyze students, we can see the massive effects of learning and practicing math. When students complete three to four digital lessons per week or about 90–120 minutes per week, they show improvements in their understanding, regardless of their starting point, race, or gender. In fact, students who struggle the most show the most gains. Math is a language, and when you practice with purpose, you learn it. It becomes intuitive. And you build a numerate mind.

Part III

THE NUMERACY IDEAL AND REALITIES

"For these are all our children. We will profit from, or pay for, what they become."

—JAMES BALDWIN

"Math literacy will be a liberation tool for people trying to get out of poverty and the best hope for people trying not to get left behind."

—ROBERT D. "BOB" MOSES

CHAPTER 10

The Equation That Will Decide Our Fate

BOTH THE DREAMS OF YOUNG PEOPLE AND THE REALity of jobs have changed dramatically over the last thirty years, moving math success from optional to a necessity. But the way we educate children hasn't changed. We dash their dreams, often before they can fully form. We have to stop doing this.

Children and young adults have many of the same, evergreen, dream jobs: doctor, teacher, veterinarian, firefighter, dancer, pilot, police officer. But there are new dream jobs in the mix, too, such as working in information technology or being a social media influencer. In a 2018 survey of students in forty-one countries, including the United States, one change noted globally was that nearly all the career aspirations of young people required postsecondary education and many required advanced degrees. We know that algebra completion in K–12 is the most predictive activity of college admission and college completion. So, said another way, the dreams of kids around the world today knowingly or unknowingly presume math success.

Observing the marketplace reality, both in the present day and considering the future of work, one notable change is the number of jobs that require secondary degrees, or technical knowledge, are increasing much faster than those that don't. Examples include being a data scientist or an electrician. In 1980, about half of those employed were in jobs that required above-average preparation, like college or technical certification, and half of those employed were in jobs that didn't. That is no longer the case. Jobs requiring advanced preparation have increased faster than those that don't. Today, the majority require advanced preparation. Further, among the top six skills employers are looking for in college graduates, half relate to mathematical thinking, including "critical thinking skills," "the ability to analyze and interpret data," and "the ability to demonstrate complex problem-solving skills."

And yet, many of the most accomplished people I talk to still view math as a luxury rather than a necessity. A few years ago, I was telling an Ivy League professor about Zearn, and in my usual fashion, I talked about our key findings, that all kids can be math kids and that we adults need to do things differently to make that happen. She interrupted me: "But you do agree that children can have many passions—ballet or soccer? We want to make room for all of those students."

Her interjection threw me off. I had been trying to explain how math can make room for everyone, and she was admonishing me for excluding some children. I was thrown off and flubbed my response. I opened my mouth to say something and then closed it without making a sound.

Afterward, I shared the story with a journalist friend, trying to understand what had gone wrong. She told me the professor and I had completely different assumptions about math: I viewed math as essential and presumed the professor did, too, but the professor saw it as a hobby or special interest—one option among many. Perhaps math was that, a long time ago. And it can still be a passion or a hobby; I know people who do long division in their heads to relax.

Personally, I never expected to be a STEM worker. I had complicated thoughts about science, technology, engineering, and math. Like many women, I stereotyped the space as a boring and uncreative grind. I thought the jobs were niche and esoteric. But I create every day, from helping to shape our software-based digital math lessons, to working on our interactive professional learning for adults, to exploring our data as we analyze how kids learn math. My work is not esoteric at all. For me, it's part of the most vital work, educating our children. As I shared earlier in this book, my childhood dreams were those of helping people; I thought that might be at the American Red Cross. Now my way of serving is as a STEM worker at Zearn.

Perhaps because I am an accidental, though delighted, STEM worker, stories of fields transforming to include

STEM and new technologies capture me. For a long time, archaeology was a field in which the discoveries were both accidental and done by hand. After stumbling upon something special, archaeologists would work meticulously, with small brushes and chisels, for years. I remember hearing the story of a boy and a dog stumbling upon a vast network of caves with elaborate paintings in the Dordogne Valley of France—the famous Lascaux. There was hard work, of course, but also a lot of luck and fortune involved. With the infusion of STEM workers and new technologies, the field of archaeology has transformed. Discoveries are now systematically accomplished. In 2022, archaeologists found a network of cities and one hundred miles of road likely built between 1000 BCE and 150 AD by scanning vast swaths of impenetrable jungle in northern Guatemala and southern Mexico using LIDAR (light detection and ranging) technology. Many believe they have discovered the first "freeway system" and transformed our understanding of ancient Mayan civilization.

More people are pursuing STEM jobs than ever before. Others are finding themselves in them unexpectedly, as I did. The US workforce is already STEM heavy at 23 percent, or roughly thirty-six million people. This is not defined by academic degree but rather by the actual work. There are only two million people with computer science degrees in the US. STEM jobs are lucrative and stable. The National Science Foundation finds that these workers tend to have both higher salaries and lower unemployment rates than their non-STEM counterparts. Median earnings for full-time, year-round workers ages twenty-five and older in STEM jobs are close to $80,000, nearly double the comparable median salary for non-STEM workers at just over $40,000.

Completing math courses is a predictor of academic and career success, and not completing them is a predictor of failure—students who don't pass algebra have only a 20 percent chance of completing high school. Yes, four out of five children who fail algebra drop out and don't complete high school. Young adults who complete college or other selective career training dramatically boost their earning potential. One recent study found that high school graduates on average earn $30,000 a year while college graduates earn $52,000 a year, or more than 40 percent higher salaries. We can even see the impact of completing specific math courses on future job earnings. As far back as 2001, when professors Heather Rose and Julian R. Betts published a study titled *Math Matters,* we knew a link existed between courses completed and income. For instance, they found that even ten years after people finished high school, those who had completed a calculus class made 65 percent more in income than other men and women who did not go beyond taking a vocational math class. This was true regardless of ethnicity, gender, and other differentiating demographics.

The pandemic has had a negative impact on K–12 math preparation and achievement. In the wake of school disruptions, NAEP (National Assessment of Educational Progress) saw its biggest drops in math scores, ever. The NAEP had shown that math scores improved a bit over the last few decades, meaning only 40 percent of fourth graders and 34 percent of eighth graders score proficiently. Post-pandemic, eighth-grade math scores fell by 8 points, bringing student performance to a level not seen since 2000. The share of students deemed proficient in eighth grade dropped from 34 percent to 26 percent, meaning that $\frac{1}{3}$ of our eighth graders used to be proficient and now it is $\frac{1}{4}$. Fourth-grade math scores fell by 5 points, similar to 2003 levels. The pandemic wiped out twenty years of math learning progress.

Looking at how we are preparing students, through the postsecondary lens, Peg Tyre in *The Atlantic* shared that from 2003 to 2009, nearly 50 percent of students who pursued a STEM degree dropped out because they found they didn't have the quantitative background they needed to succeed. As a result, those who do persist in math and related STEM disciplines in the United States often come from abroad. More than half of computer science PhD students come from outside the country, and temporary visa holders represented close to 40 percent of doctoral degree earners in science and engineering in 2019.

There is a huge mismatch. Educational achievement, particularly in mathematics, is not improving as fast as our young peoples' ambitions are growing. Math achievement is also not improving as fast as today's job market requires, let alone what the future of work needs. We could change that. While there are many levers for building the workforce of the future, including improving social and emotional skills, one necessary lever is to ensure that all kids are successful in K–12 math. But this point is still considered frustratingly controversial. Math is still for math kids rather than for everyone.

Today, math is the language of the world around us. Some can speak it and some can't. Those without numeracy are cut off from crucial understanding of life and society, and from vital opportunities. Success in math predicts many positive outcomes. We should not pretend otherwise. But in math education, we are collectively pretending; this is otherwise known as a delusion. We are missing two sets of information: the facts on how numeracy is required for a good job and how numeracy connects to your day-to-day life and allows you to navigate it successfully.

Perhaps you know an adult who can't balance his checkbook or figure out the tip on a restaurant bill. Maybe you struggle with filing your taxes or creating a savings plan. Perhaps you find your insurance bills perplexing or can't understand the implications of new financial laws and regulations.

We live in a world where financial literacy is far more relevant than it was in the past. Gone are the days when most people retire with pensions—learning how to save for retirement requires some serious math forecasting skills. Living on a budget, too, is much more a challenge than it used to be, given much shorter job longevity and a larger percentage of people working for themselves in the gig economy (and not receiving a regular paycheck). People are also investing online rather than putting money in savings accounts or using a broker. More math knowledge is needed to discern a good investment from someone trying to fleece you.

Consider the 2007–08 financial crisis, also known as the Great Recession and the Global Financial Crisis. There's a reason this event has been given such dramatic names. Between 2007 and 2010, the median net worth of families fell precipitously from $126,400 to $77,300. This set American households back to 1992 levels. One major source of fuel to the crisis was widespread defaults on home loans that had adjustable rates instead of fixed rates. In America, home buyers have access to a thirty-year fixed-rate mortgage. Typically, the buyer would put 20 percent down, borrow 80 percent from the bank, and then pay interest and principal to the bank each month. If a person bought a $200,000 home, they'd put down $40,000 and borrow $160,000. If the thirty-year fixed rate was 5 percent, they would pay $859 per month, allowing a family to own a home even if they didn't have $200,000 in cash.

But during the lead-up to the Great Recession, lenders experimented with new loan structures that the public, regulators, and likely the lenders themselves did not have the mathematical intuition to properly evaluate. (Remember that 22 percent of US eighth-grade students score proficient on the NAEP exam.) Banks offered deals on adjustable rate mortgages, or ARMs, with a very low teaser introductory rate. So you might have a loan that was 1 percent for the first year, 2 percent for years two and three, and then the rate would jump to 10 percent per year. That would mean your payments on that same $160,000 loan for your $200,000 house would be $515 a month in the first year, then $591 a month, and then, one morning, $1,404. That's the morning you would default. Six million American households lost their homes to foreclosure during the Global Financial Crisis. Many had not calculated that they were in homes they could not afford. Further, when six million homeowners default, bringing the whole financial system down with them, there are catastrophic math-understanding issues from top to bottom.

When I shared some statistics with a business executive about the poor job we are doing teaching math to kids, he responded, "This is why people are getting cheated out of their money." He was referring to people being scammed by investment fraud and other schemers, and he was right. With broad-based numeracy, we can build a society of people who are capable of protecting one another. Financial literacy lessons are shown to help as well, when they are additive to widespread numeracy, not a substitute for it. For example, lessons on how insurance or a mortgage works require a strong working knowledge of rates and percentages—ideas that should be mastered in seventh and eighth grade.

A range of problems that might seem disconnected are the result of undereducating our kids, specifically in the world of mathematics. Conversely, a lot of problems will be solved when we build a numerate generation. The greater the numeracy, the more likely that we'll produce a population capable of solving environmental, technological, health, and other societal problems. Unlocking everyone's potential wouldn't just increase the proportion of engineers coming up with answers to our most pressing problems—it would break down the wall between STEM and other fields of expertise, and produce a society where everyone has the ability and power to engage with the technological and quantitative questions around them, so that different domains of knowledge can work together.

There is no question that a great deal of technology innovation is superficial, and misleadingly labeled innovation at all. But technical and scientific breakthroughs are necessary to solve our hardest problems. For example, one of the primary barriers to scaling renewable energy sources such as wind and solar is called the Green Premium. Basically, in many cases it costs more to use green energy sources than fossil fuels. As Bill Gates shares in his book *How to Avoid a Climate Disaster*, "The main culprits are our demand for reliability, and the curse of intermittency." The sun does not shine nor does the wind blow twenty-four hours a day, but we consume electricity twenty-four hours a day. So the hardest nut to crack in moving renewable energy forward in an efficient and effective way is what to do when the sun or wind are not powering our grid. One solution could be cheap, large batteries. If we can solve the technological challenges to have large, cheap batteries or other means to store excess solar and wind energy, we could start to tip the scales to where renewable energy will be cheaper than fossil fuels.

If we had an army of young people with the mathematical and technical skills to explore and tinker with this renewable energy problem, we would answer it sooner. Many of the climate and energy concerns are problems of innovation. We simply need more humans with the preparation in mathematics working to find new answers. Just like batteries, treating cancer, reducing income inequality, and getting clean drinking water to every human, each goal has innovation and technical challenges that need to be solved.

Though I am a math evangelist, and I spend more time than you would even guess thinking about and solving K–8 math problems, I know that math is not a panacea. But math success is now a critical ingredient for our success. Math offers knowledge and skills that are especially relevant to a time when we require more critical thinking and problem-solving than ever before.

I used to dream that I would hear leaders and politicians wax enthusiastic about math education. Like the dogs that don't bark, I have often lamented the absence. But things are starting to change.

After working in the world of math education for more than a decade, in the winter of 2022, I observed a shift. Here's a sample, amalgamated like a restaurant review, of what leaders are saying on math education:

"Giving every child access to a quality education—regardless of their race or income—is the civil rights issue of our day"; "it made us the best-educated, best-prepared nation in the world, but the world has caught up"; "although there are many factors that affect a student's trajectory, the evidence shows that it's extremely important for them to succeed in math"; "to help improve achievement, we are proposing new investments in high-quality math curricula and training to ensure that our educators have the support they need to help all our students thrive"; "a student that has notable gaps in primary grades mathematics proficiency . . . will not be successful in algebra . . . we are dependent upon our kids today learning . . . not to mention the moral obligation we have to each of the five and a half million souls in our system to give them our absolute best."

This enthusiasm is necessary, and we need more. It must be channeled into effective efforts to build the broad-based numeracy that will enrich everyone's lives and will build a healthy, successful, math-informed society. The need for numeracy is now.

CHAPTER 11

Teach Our Children Well

WE ALL HAVE A ROLE IN CREATING A NUMERATE society—parents, teachers, school administrators, sports coaches, journalists, filmmakers, business leaders, and policymakers. But to get there, the numeracy revolution needs the same passion and purpose of the worldwide literacy movement, which in the United States has been resparked with stories of the "Mississippi miracle" and the blockbuster podcast *Sold a Story.* What is animating this moment is the captivating yet believable idea that all kids can learn and love reading. When it comes to math, we need more pop culture touchstones that tell stories of redemption—children who struggled until they succeeded, adults who are thriving in jobs that rely on math, even if they weren't "math kids" themselves. We need business leaders and politicians talking about how critical—and attainable—math education is for *all* our kids. Educators and parents need to provide the right type of support to generate enthusiasm and curiosity rather than disengagement with, or hatred for, the subject.

Perhaps by now you're on board, but you're still asking, "What should I do?" Let's start where we all first learn to learn: at home.

How to Raise a Math-Loving, Math-Learning Kid

Families model behaviors that have profound effects on their children, from nutrition to money mindsets. What we say and do relative to math will influence our kids' attitudes toward and success in math classes, from parents and siblings to aunties, uncles, and grandparents. I attended college with two of my cousins, both of whom helped me navigate undergrad, helping me pick classes based on my passions or giving me advice on how to negotiate a double major. Chosen families count as well. Growing up, my parents built a family of dear friends who had also immigrated from India in the 1960s and 1970s. A few of those aunties and uncles were as essential as blood relations in creating my sense of self as a learner and encouraging me to take advanced coursework in math even though I was one of a handful of girls in the class. Their support bolstered my courage.

If you're a parent, you may be unaware of how your words and deeds affect your kids and inadvertently make them feel that they lack ability or that doing math is drudgery. One of my favorite moments in *The Simpsons* is an exchange between Bart Simpson's mom, Marge, and the superintendent of Springfield's school district: "We have reason to believe your son is dealing drugs." "Dealing drugs? That's impossible; he doesn't have the math skills."

But you can also provide the encouragement and take specific actions to help your children fulfill their potential. The goal isn't to transform your child into a math savant who'll grow up to solve some obscure proof no one has yet cracked, like the Riemann hypothesis. (If solved, it may reveal the pattern of prime numbers . . . and it comes with a million-dollar prize.) Instead, it's to provide an environment and support that fosters an appreciation and understanding of math.

Parents have a number of tools at their disposal to achieve this goal, but let's start with the first prerequisite: positive math consciousness. This means approaching math with a mindset unburdened by the myths I discussed earlier. More specifically, it means understanding three basic math truths and keeping them in mind when your child has trouble on a test or asks for help with homework.

First, struggle is a natural part of the math learning process. Don't panic if your child is having problems with their assignments. Making mistakes is normal. Math can be challenging, and even the most passionate minds mess up their calculations. If your child strikes out or muffs a ground ball during softball practice, you wouldn't tell her that she's no good at it and should quit. Accept that mistakes are not an assessment of whether your child can succeed but an inevitable and useful part of the learning process. How do you encourage your child to continue to participate in an after-school team if practice went poorly? Do you let them give up or do you offer perspective? Do you pity and coddle them or feel grateful that they are learning a vital life lesson? Bring all those mindsets and strategies to your child's math learning.

Second, repeat the affirmation *Every kid is a math kid.* From ten years of building Zearn and helping millions of students do billions of math problems, I know it's true, even for those who have fallen behind their classmates and are classified as below grade level. With a combination of grade-level learning and just-in-time support of foundational learning, students who've fallen behind are able to catch up with their peers. Just as everyone can learn to read, everyone can learn to do math. This truth should help you develop a positive attitude toward your child's prospects—an attitude that kids can sense loud and clear.

Third, math proficiency is a prerequisite for success today. Math is the language of our tech-dependent, digital world. In a memorable scene in the movie classic *Peggy Sue Got Married,* the protagonist, played by Kathleen Turner, dismisses algebra as useless. I can't explain why that scene has stayed with me, but it's even more wrong today than it was when the movie was made in 1986. Numeracy is necessary for everyone.

By keeping these three truths in mind, you'll find it easier to implement the following suggestions:

- Make it simple. Math is everywhere, and you can show it to your children in innumerable ways. Play cards and board games. It doesn't matter whether it's Monopoly or gin rummy, Chutes and Ladders or a favorite in our household, Rummikub. A range of board games and most card games require math, so pick ones that you and your children enjoy and make them part of your family routine. Don't overthink it and definitely don't overtalk it. There's no faster way to take the fun out of game night than by turning it into a pontificating lesson. Enjoy the games as designed and let the learning and enjoyment flow naturally as the kids count whether they have enough cash to put another house on Marvin Gardens.

- Engage kids in math discussions that emerge both organically and authentically. Don't deliver lectures about the importance of math, or drill nonstop on multiplication tables (and don't try to buy their compliance with sugary snacks). Math is all around us—when we pay a bill at a restaurant, when we're trying to figure out the size of carpet to get for a room, or when a child wants to know how long it will take him to save enough money to pay for a new toy. When my twins were younger, we went to the farmers market on weekends and

I'd give them $10 each and ask them to buy our fruits and vegetables, and to calculate the change before paying. Just being in charge of the cash made this activity exciting enough that they begged to do it each week. This is what I mean by organic and authentic—we all need groceries, so it's not a fake task that kids sniff out instantly and then come to resent.

- Use high-quality free resources. The internet is a terrific resource for fun and effective math instruction, but you have to be discerning. Obviously, I'm biased—my kids use Zearn. We eat the cooking. Khan Academy is another high-quality free resource that I let them explore. Beware of programs that replicate the old failures of math teaching, with oversimplified algorithms that take kids back to second-grade purgatory if they make a few mistakes on a fourth-grade problem. Look for digital tools that *teach* students when they make a mistake and set them up for the same rigorous challenge when they try again, as opposed to those that take away the challenge, along with learning and ultimately curiosity.

- When your children struggle or fall behind, partner with the school. (Remember, struggle and mistakes are a natural part of the process.) Ask their teachers: Can we develop a plan to help my child catch up to grade level? This means providing a plan to supply the learning that they're missing and supporting them to continue to learn grade-level math so they don't fall further behind. Yes, this often means spending extra time on math.

Those are the "dos" but there are also some "don'ts." Too often, when parents want to help their children master math, they don't realize that their words or actions are counterproductive. Here are three key things to avoid:

- Don't tell your children that they're not the only ones who dislike math. I know you're just trying to make them feel better after they struggled with a problem or did poorly on a test. But the road to math hell is paved with good intentions. If you have a child who refuses to eat her fruits and vegetables, do you try to make her feel better about this issue by telling her that other kids don't like fruits and vegetables? If anything, take it in the opposite direction. When my children were little, I pretended everyone loved vegetables and fought to eat them. I told my kids that my friends used to steal my vegetables. Let's do the same here. Tell them everyone *loves* math. Once they enter the larger world, they are going to constantly hear negative views on math. Provide a bit of a counterweight at home.

- Don't let your own insecurities or beliefs about math interfere with your child's learning. If you hated math and weren't successful at it, don't pass along that hatred and perception of incompetence. And as much as I don't like my next point, it's validated by research: Moms need to be especially vigilant about passing on their math insecurities to their sons and daughters because they are more likely than dads to commit this error. That's because a mother is more likely than a father to identify as "not a math person," which is not helpful to your kids. (If it's any comfort, moms also are more likely than dads to pass on positive attitudes about learning generally.)

- Don't communicate that math is a special interest. For instance: "You don't have to be good at everything; you're such a wonderful artist. Math is something that only a few kids are really good at." Be conscious of how you speak about math, and if you find yourself lapsing into special-interest language, remind yourself to discuss it in the same way you talk about reading—how it's a necessary subject for everyone to master and love.

The Educational Challenge

When it comes to teaching math, schools face an obstacle that doesn't exist for other subjects. They're not only battling the attitudes parents and older siblings of students may have passed on (consciously or not) but biases from television shows and movies. I've referenced *Peggy Sue Got Married,* in which adult Peggy Sue gets magically transported back to high school. Let's examine the scene that is seared into my brain:

Friend: "Peggy Sue, did you study for the test?"

Peggy Sue: "Test! There is a test!"

Peggy Sue doodles on her paper during the test and hands it in to the teacher when the time is up.

Teacher: "And what's the meaning of this, Peggy Sue?"

Peggy Sue: "Uh, Mr. Snellgrove, I happen to know in the future I will not have the slightest use for algebra and I speak from experience."

Bell rings. Students laugh and applaud.

Here is the result of countless shows and movies that convey the same message: math phobia. The math test is terrifying, and Peggy Sue is terrified. In the years since she was in high school, she's forgotten whatever math she'd once memorized—the underlying premise being that it was a random and meaningless set of procedures. Peggy Sue, as an intelligent adult of means, presumably has learned to do all sorts of life-math tasks—balance a checkbook, figure out the dimensions of rooms in her house, manage the household budget. But she doesn't tell herself, "I know the basic rules of base 10 and I know how equations balance, so I should give this test a go." She declares that math is pointless, the other students applaud, and the audience nods along.

In real life, fortunately, we've made a good deal of progress fighting this phobia. From professors at top universities to elementary school teachers, instructors at various grade levels recognize that math phobia exists and that certain teaching methods—taking chairs out of a math classroom and making students stand to emphasize that math instruction is for weeding out weak performers—make a bad situation worse. They understand this message of scarcity and exclusion can be especially harmful to phobia-vulnerable students—those who may not have STEM role models, including girls and Black and Latino students.

Long gone are the days, mostly, when a math teacher acted like a drill instructor ("Only a few of you will make it through!"). Math teachers I meet around the country are deeply interested in creating learning opportunities. Many of them grew up in that old-fashioned culture and are committed to ending it.

Teachers and school administrators should also understand that students fear math when they can't grasp a problem intuitively. This means that the problem doesn't make sense to them, and when something doesn't make sense, they experience disequilibrium and can't figure out what's required. Even students who are good at math can become math-phobic if they lack an intuitive grasp of a concept or problem. The Cornell University mathematician Steven Strogatz has discussed his fear of math when he was a college freshman studying linear algebra. His teacher didn't help him understand the subject, and he became nervous before tests, struggled with the homework, and received a poor grade. As he shared in a *Freakonomics* podcast, "I got very discouraged and thought maybe I didn't have the right stuff to be a math major. . . . What was missing from that first course was intuition. It wasn't visual enough. I couldn't picture what was happening."

The challenge for teachers is to find a balance between building fluency, creating understanding, and applying both in problem-solving. A lack of fluency—not being able to automatically rely on foundational math facts—can become an obstacle to learning. As the Strogatz example illustrates, a lack of understanding or application prevents us from approaching math with our intuition. Any of these "lacks" can create math phobia. Teachers must aim for the sweet spot of doing all three.

The good news is that we're making progress when it comes to teaching math in a better way. Schools and teachers throughout this country and the world are recognizing the value of pictures and intuition to help students love what they learn. At work, we conducted a study of 345,000 third- to fifth-grade students on math engagement. When we asked them if it was important for them to do well at math, 93 percent of those surveyed responded affirmatively—including the majority of students who said they "do not like" or that they "hate" math. Unlike Peggy Sue, these students recognize the value of math in their lives.

The growing interest in and positive attitude toward math is due in large part to how the digital world has mastered conveying complex ideas in pictures. When I played the popular educational game Oregon Trail as a kid, before the makers had created their Graphical User Interface, this is what the screen looked like:

CDC Cyber 70

```
?2

BAD LUCK---YOUR DAUGHTER BROKE HER ARM
YOU HAD TO STOP AND USE SUPPLIES TO
MAKE A SLING

MONDAY JUNE 7 1847

TOTAL MILEAGE IS 929
FOOD   BULLETS   CLOTHING   SUPPLIES   CASH
 53      1782       69          75        0

DO YOU WANT TO
  (1) STOP AT THE NEXT FORT
  (2) HUNT
  (3) CONTINUE
?2
TYPE BANG: BANG
RIGHT BETWEEN THE EYES
---YOU GOT A BIG ONE!!!!

DO YOU WANT TO EAT
(1) POORLY (2) MODERATELY OR (3) WELL
?
```

(Image credit: Gameloft S.A.)

This game was hard to understand and was not intuitive. It was difficult to get started and have fun. You had to imagine what was happening as you set out westward in 1848, typing fluorescent green letters onto a black screen. The updated Oregon Trail is filled with compelling visuals. Instead of writing alphanumeric commands, my sons use a touch screen to move images of people and supplies from place to place. Similar visual elements help build students' math intuition. Many of us who teach take a cue from the digital world and use graphical interfaces to present math in pictures and through visualizations. One change that has resulted from this more image-oriented approach is that children as young as six or seven start drawing sophisticated math pictures when they're confused by a problem or concept. I've also seen many third graders drawing as they work, and sixth graders creating ratio tables as they grapple with proportional reasoning.

How do you bring visual, intuitive materials into math teaching? Here I would offer two ideas that are really one. Use high-quality instructional resources in your teaching (physical or digital) that support intuition, and take out resources that don't. At the simplest level, intuition is built and supported with visualizations or the concrete to pictorial to abstract framework.

When it comes to teaching with pictures, don't get carried away! Seeing visuals helps students quickly understand concepts, but forcing them to draw can become tedious. Recall the plates of cookies from earlier. Showing kids three plates with seven cookies each gives them an immediate insight into the meaning of $3 \times 7 = 21$. That doesn't mean you need to keep making them draw twenty-one cookies, especially once they have reached fluency and know the answer. A middle ground exists that stimulates intuition without stupefying students.

What We All Can Do

To build math sense for everyone, we need to change the narrative outside the classroom as well. Too many movies, stories, idioms, and jokes frame math as a form of human torture, or present success as a rare, inborn gift. Push back when you hear a negative narrative. Of course, math is hard, as is nearly everything worthwhile in life. Students will make mistakes. Mistakes are required to learn. Math is worth it. It is the equation that will decide our fate.

CHAPTER 12

From Sorting to Teaching

MATH MATTERS FOR EVERYONE, BUT WE ACT AS IF IT matters only for a select few. Our education system is built around both overt and quiet classifying of students—what I have referred to as sorting. We track classes, placing the "math whizzes" in advanced courses, the "slower" kids in classes with euphemistic names: introductory, basic, general. We administer diagnostics that tell students through their scores and subsequent work what we think of their abilities. Those who are taken off the fast track don't "go at their own pace"; instead, they never really get to learn at all.

While I know that no administrators or teachers intend to communicate to children that they're math dunces, the teaching and learning system we have designed sends them that message anyway. They're chastised for doing the problem the wrong way, confusing them further. If they draw pictures, they are told not to. They come to believe that because they can't solve a problem quickly, the problem isn't for them. There is someone else who can solve it in under a minute, so why try?

Ultimately, children don't have to be told they're bad at math; they tell themselves. They sort themselves out based on the accumulation of negative messages they've received. Further, the sorting system is so crushing, even for those who get sorted into the math pile, that we extinguish their curiosity for math altogether.

That's the bad news.

The good news is that we can all be math people if we change the goal of instruction from sorting to teaching. We came up with this system; we can design a better one.

I founded Zearn based on two propositions: Digital tools could democratize access to an excellent education, and technology could find ways to complement the work of teaching and learning. When we started testing these propositions, however, I realized that we knew little about how children learn mathematics. There was no manual for what we wanted to do. While finding a path, I discovered that the most interesting answers were to the questions I had not initially asked.

The most meaningful of these questions, so far, has been this: In math, why are we allocating so much time, money, and energy to sorting when we could be teaching?

I am not a magical thinker. I know that the average height of an NBA player is six feet six and the average height of a man in the United States is five feet eight. In fact, the 99th percentile for a man in the United States is only six feet four. Not every kid can grow up to play in the NBA. Talent, passion, perseverance—and genetic features such as height—naturally sort the people who have a future in professional basketball.

In some areas of STEM, we need NBA-level talent and dedication from the mathematicians innovating to write the first natural language processing algorithms that give us generative AI, and engineers sorting out quantum computing. But we don't all have to be LeBron James. Working for more than ten years in this field makes me confident that all kids can learn and love math. Just because they're unlikely to make it to the NBA doesn't discourage millions of kids from playing and loving a pickup game with friends. Succeeding in algebra is like playing sports recreationally. It's challenging, it's fun, and we can all do it.

In many discussions around math talent and teaching, people talk as if it's necessary to choose between cultivating exceptional NBA-level talent or making numeracy widespread. But it's not either-or. We can raise the floor of achievement, raise the ceiling of passion and talent, and move up everything in between.

This idea that we can't do it all assumes that to achieve the goal of widespread numeracy, we must dumb down the way we teach, sabotaging elite achievement. It treats math education as a scarce resource, so that making all kids math kids would interfere with supporting the extraordinary passion and talent of a few. Unfortunately, this scarcity mindset has taken hold. With only 35 percent of fourth graders and 25 percent of eighth graders reaching proficiency in mathematics, we aren't even giving most kids the chance to find out if they might thrive.

How do we make the transition from scarcity to abundance, from selecting an elite minority for math careers to democratizing the experience of learning math? In short, from sorting to teaching? I've shared how my reflections on this question have evolved in my decade in the field, and I hope it provides a useful process for helping you make the mindset shift, too. I started by examining the math myths and then searched for reality-based methods to help kids learn and love math. I drew on research, firsthand experience, and a dataset of millions of students completing billions of problems.

Sorting is deeply ingrained in teaching and learning mathematics because it has been our only option for most of human history. Hundreds of years ago, a town would be lucky to have a few people who could read, write, and do basic math. These individuals had many critical jobs in the functioning of the town. For example, they might be in charge of rationing the winter stores of grain to last till the spring harvest for the whole community.

In addition, they were the only teachers who could pass on their academic knowledge to the children of the town. They were busy people! Due to the scarcity of these humans and their time in any given location, the only rational choice was to pick a few children to learn with the scholars. It wasn't until recently that we had enough schools, teachers, books, writing implements, or other instructional materials, including digital tools, to go around (and many places still don't). Because the scarcity was so extreme, we could not envision a world of abundance in resources.

To move toward widespread numeracy, we need to undo the work that built these systems. Nearly everything about the way we teach math still rests on this foundation. Although I have spent more than a decade turning myself away from the sorting mindset and actions, I still catch myself stumbling into it.

Rebuilding math instruction around teaching *everyone* is the only way to create a critical mass of math-proficient people to solve the world's problems. When I view my job from a teaching perspective, I ask a couple of crucial questions to assess what we're doing when we teach mathematics: *Why do I believe this? Why am I choosing this course of action? Does this rest on math success being about sorting or about learning?*

Renounce the Myths and Embrace the Methods

The first step is to be vigilant about renouncing the myths of math instruction. These beliefs are the mechanisms and justifications of sorting. They're why children learn to hate math and learn that math hates them back. The experience of being sorted, or worse, humiliated, under these premises is what extinguishes math curiosity.

To renounce the myths, you need to state the opposite realities, as follows:

Speed isn't everything. As I've noted, automaticity—the ability to call upon key facts and skills quickly and reflexively—is vital in math. When we have automaticity or fluency of math facts and procedures, we free up working memory to apply to the hard math problem in front of us. Timed activities help build up this capability.

But speed kills . . . fun and creativity. If you know an engineer, a programmer, or a scientist, ask them about how long it took them to figure out a recent work problem. I guarantee they'll tell you that they spent days, weeks, months, and even years working out solutions. Speed is only one essential tool in math learning to provide a specific benefit, and overemphasizing it leads to neglecting the others—reducing rigor and increasing math anxiety.

Speed gets emphasized because it's such a lazy tool for sorting. Making math a series of sprints makes it easy to declare winners and losers. Even worse, it ends up convincing students to sort themselves, on the belief that the whole field of math learning is only for the fastest seven- and eight-year-olds in basic addition and multiplication.

As we have seen, more-advanced math students (such as graduate students in physics) move more slowly through problem-solving than less-advanced math students (say, undergrads with one course in physics). They've learned to see more in the problems to pay attention to. Overemphasizing speed also makes math boring. Doing fast math becomes like practicing scales on the piano without ever playing a melody.

Tricks are not the answer. Math is a set of axioms or rules of the universe that you can trust completely. But we often teach it as a set of arbitrary-seeming, unconnected tricks. When you memorize tricks to solve problems, you are robbed of the intrinsic joy that comes from solving a puzzle, everything clicking into place. Even worse, memorizing tricks causes critical thinking skills to atrophy. Instead of sharpening your intuition and reasoning, you default to hacks.

Algorithms are not tricks. The standard addition algorithm always works whether you are adding two-digit numbers or ten-digit numbers, whereas the "bow tie method" for adding fractions will let you down quickly once you move beyond two addends. Tricks expire, making math something you can't trust. Algorithms always work. Because they always work, algorithms have a clear internal logic. Teaching math as a set of tricks—even presenting algorithms as tricks to execute rather than processes to understand—prevents students from having the chance to see that logic. It assumes math is too difficult for them, and sorts out the majority of students into a pile of people who can't be expected to understand what's on the board.

There is no single way. You've been conditioned to believe that there is one correct or proper way to solve a problem. Reject this conditioning. Be open-minded and exploratory rather than single-minded and reactive when faced with a math problem. Consider the difference between answer-getting and problem-solving. Answer-getting is when math is taught as a rigid set of steps to follow. Students suspend intuition, creativity, and understanding to follow the steps. When they do get the answer, they often aren't sure if it's right or wrong; they have no number sense about the problem. They go through the process disempowered, with no chance to understand. Answer-getting doesn't allow you to explore other ways of solving the problem or prepare you for real-world problem-solving.

Problem-solving is a creative cognitive process in which you strive to deepen your understanding. There are many ways to solve a problem, and they usually require visualizing it. In real-world STEM contexts, engineers discuss many ways of attacking a problem before they even begin their work. Their goal may be to find a more elegant, cheaper, or faster approach. The myth that there's a single way to solve a math problem keeps people from ever experiencing this process. It's another sorting and self-sorting mechanism, in which students aren't given the chance to use their inborn ability to think mathematically.

My experiences at Zearn have convinced me that we have a social and moral obligation to move from sorting to teaching. To do this, after we've learned what not to believe about math, we need to understand what to do about it. Though we are still learning how to teach math collectively, we now know enough methods to improve our teaching efficacy. These are the methods that build problem-solving ability and spark interest—reviving mathematical curiosity when it has been suppressed, or, for our youngest children who haven't run the gauntlet of self-sorting, fueling that curiosity from the beginning.

I've discussed some of the methods we can use to achieve this goal, and I'd also like to share how these methods can help take us from a sorting to a teaching approach:

Know you belong. When the math classroom is inclusive, fostering a sense of belonging, kids don't automatically classify themselves as the have-nots. Because the broader societal narrative fosters a negative math identity as normal, letting kids know they belong is the lever we can lean on to shift our collective consciousness, opening space for more children and adults to succeed in math. When kids make mistakes, they and their teachers need to understand it's not a signal they don't belong but a sign they're in the right place: making mistakes is a feature of learning math, an indicator that learning is happening. Students need to feel belonging frequently in math, especially when the learning becomes challenging. As we ask students to push through each new challenge, they need the scaffold of belonging.

Use pictures and objects. Objects and math pictures give concrete meaning to deep mathematical ideas, for kids and adults alike. People respond to seeing the concept of multiplication translated into plates and chocolate chip cookies, as we saw earlier. When you present math strictly in terms of numerals and symbols, most concepts don't make intuitive sense. The kids who can't get them are sorted out.

Using pictures and objects as well as abstract symbols allows us to understand as well as compute efficiently. Adults sometimes tell me that they would hide or erase their math pictures as kids because they believed that was "cheating" or a sign they weren't good at math. The truth was the opposite. They were building their mathematical intuition by tapping into the way the human brain works. Explaining math using representations as well as abstract language is not only for elementary school. It must be a part of learning each time we encounter a new challenge, even as adults. If we really want to stop sorting and start promoting widespread understanding, then using pictures and objects, as well as abstract symbols, must be a part of both the core math block and the extended times such as tutoring or summer school.

Make an easier problem. No one should have to give you permission to make a problem easier—it ought to be treated as common sense. This method speaks volumes about how the system sorts. Students who succeed at math often have been taught to make easier problems. They have been given permission to go rogue, while students who come to mistrust math have been forbidden to do it. If I told you to walk around in circles to get from point A to B instead of going in a straight line, you would assume I was crazy and not listen. But the gatekeepers have gaslighted us to make it feel as if we should embrace the counterintuitive, harder way. For example, completing a dozen procedural calculations when drawing a quick picture is a faster way to determine which fraction is closest in value. Making an easier problem does not mean shortchanging the learning. In fact, making an easier problem like the five ways I shared to find the product of 35 × 18 improves learning. Exploring other ways to solve a problem builds and hones problem-solving skills.

Try a different way. If kids think there's only one way to solve a problem, and that way doesn't work for them, they automatically assume it's over, and nothing else will work. "Something is wrong with me," they think. "I can't do math."

That is the voice of sorting that they hear, echoing from the educational system, from familes, from all of us. We assume the worst, too; we take them out of the grade-level math they are working on and drop them to lower levels to reduce their struggle, thinking we can catch them up on some earlier learning they left unfinished. As a result, they are now behind on the new learning. If we keep doing this, they will be perpetually playing catch-up (and never succeeding).

We've found that students who are steered back to remedial, lower-level math problems stay behind their peers and show less improvement when they return to the topics they had originally struggled with. The solution is to help children catch up and move forward in their math learning when they first start to struggle, by bringing the targeted support to their grade-level work. But to make this change in math learning, it requires us to stop thinking of problems as a yes-or-no sorting device and start thinking of them as learning opportunities.

Practice with purpose. Endless drills lack immediate purpose or benefit. Kids learn to hate them, and from there to hate math itself. It's hard to be motivated about college and career, or even the rest of your math education, while doing thirty unrelated long division problems on a worksheet. We don't ask children to do this in other subject areas. We don't ask kids to read appliance manuals to improve their reading fluency. Not only does practice without purpose dull their motivation, it increases the speed with which children sort themselves out of math.

We hold on to the idea that math learning has to be rationed even as the means and opportunities to learn keep proliferating. Education technology has increased our abundance—overwhelming, disappointing, and delighting us. Videos and apps to learn and practice practically anything are but a few clicks away. I am even more optimistic about edtech's full potential to further democratize access to an excellent education because we are in early innings with lots of development ahead. This is why I am so excited about the work of Zearn and other edtech organizations. We're complementing the work of teachers and students at scale, using the tools of technology to expand what was once the domain of a sorted few.

Most recently, artificial intelligence, specifically generative AI such as ChatGPT, has taken the stage, perhaps overhyped or not hyped enough. If built into educational technology platforms, generative AI offers the potential for further abundance in learning, an abundance of step-change scale and capacity we can't comprehend. Educators and technologists in partnership will need to determine how to do that well.

The most salient thing to remember about both education technology and embedded generative AI is that there is not a default setting of good or evil, progress or harm, or sorting or teaching. Technology is simply a force multiplier of the goals of those who build it, even when the creators can't state the goals. The only way to produce the first fully numerate generation is to make that the organizing goal of education technology, both the technology we currently have and the technology we're still dreaming up.

Educators need to demand tools that complement their teaching, that reignite curiosity for math learning, and that build students' problem-solving capacity rather than enabling rote practice. One of the few silver linings to the dark cloud that pandemic disruptions cast over learning was this: Educators have begun to demand more from education technology. Part of these demands include an insistence that technology break the paradigm of sorting in math education.

Edtech should not increase the gaps between the haves and have-nots, as technology often does. But left to its own devices and without the vision of educators, leaders, and citizens, edtech and generative AI may actually just replicate the sorting system in math, harden it, and finally amplify it.

I already see places where this is happening. Much of the

first wave of educational technology I encounter is built to follow the sorting model. When a student gets a question wrong, they offer only limited help, usually giving a "hint" that tells or shows the answer, not how to get there. Other sorting features include overly simplified sixty-question diagnostics, which claim to assess whether a child can learn an entire grade level. If students struggle on the diagnostic, they're likely to go down the chute of remedial education. Rather than the software providing more support on grade-level math, the diagnostic sends the student into below grade-level math for weeks if not the entire academic year, ensuring they remain perpetually behind.

Even more worrisome, beautiful snippets of digital learning content exist behind a high paywall model accessible only to wealthy parents. Content creators need to be paid for their work, but great education has to be for all. Payment mechanisms should enable this. There are so many ways to do this. Teachers and parents can and do access Zearn for free for their children. (To ensure our nonprofit is sustainable, we charge schools for services we offer to the adults.)

The dreams of edtech should be bold. It must further democratize access to an excellent education, to deploy the abundance to teach all children many things, math among them. So far, we have seen that education technology can do many jobs to support the work of teaching and learning including: (1) scaling up quality instruction for children or adults through high-quality videos and sometimes adaptive videos; (2) increasing opportunities to practice, and the quality of practice, by offering more access to practice sets and real-time feedback; (3) increasing learner engagement through gamification and visualizations; (4) creating opportunities for differentiation by allowing students to go at their own pace through rigorous, not remedial, content; (5) allowing for a learner to pursue self-exploration.

When I worked at Bain & Company, I had three books at my desk that I would open and refer to when I was confused: my old textbooks from statistics, accounting, and finance. They were large, heavy, and hard to maneuver. I would wander the table of contents and indices to answer questions I could barely formulate.

Now I can enter a sentence fragment into a search bar and find a beautiful video, and in this new world of math beyond the textbook, I usually learn something I had not known before. That is abundance. I am learning math in my forties! When we were building Zearn eighth grade, I learned why $3^0 = 1$ or $N^0 = 1$. I had simply memorized that any nonzero number raised to the zero power was equal to one. I never even considered the why. Three divided by three is one. And when we raise a number to the power of zero, that is what we are saying, the number divided by itself.

$3^{1-1=0} = 1$ ↙ !

$3^0 = 1$ ↙ ?? $\frac{3^1}{3^1} = 1$ ↙ !!

$\frac{N^1}{N^1} = 1$ ↙ !!!

My twelve-year-old boys have grown up in this abundance. Recently, our family went to India, and one of my twins came back wanting to know Hindi at my level of proficiency. I told him that he had to learn to read and write, but that Hindi was easy to learn because the spelling for every word is consistent. We didn't speak about it further, but within a few weeks, he had found Duolingo and was on an impressive streak. He can already read easy words.

Meanwhile, his brother got excited about a challenge at school to learn the locations of all 195 countries on Earth. He found a game called Stack the Countries that he plays to build and master his knowledge by continent. These are all free resources. For kids who have grown up in this abundance, they presume there's enough learning material to go around. They expect to have access to learning, not to be sorted away from it. If we get lost on our journey as adults from sorting to teaching, the younger generations can show us the way.

A Window to Beauty and Awe

Every child (and adult) can be successful learning mathematics. To date, we have designed and built a system that emphasizes sorting which people get the chance to learn math. It's time to design and build a new system to teach everyone math.

I often wonder how we will know when we have done it. What will it look like? And what will it feel like?

Some of the outcomes will be measurable. We should be able to see better scores on standardized tests and, much more far-reaching, people qualified for better jobs.

I think we will see something else as well. We will know we have arrived when we regularly get to feel the transcendent beauty of math. Math is the awe-inspiring beauty of the universe itself. I realize that's not how most of us are used to discussing math, but it's the same feeling that you get when you read a transporting novel that encapsulates the whole human experience within its pages.

While I often felt the delight of solving a math problem as a kid, a few moments were different. In those moments, I felt I could touch the truth of the universe. The first was in elementary school when my dad showed me that area could be calculated by multiplying the two side lengths of a rectangle. On a paper place mat in the Pizza Hut on Transit Road in Buffalo, New York, he sketched a rectangle neatly on a place mat and labeled the sides. He then drew lines through it like this:

Then we counted the boxes. There were fifteen of them!

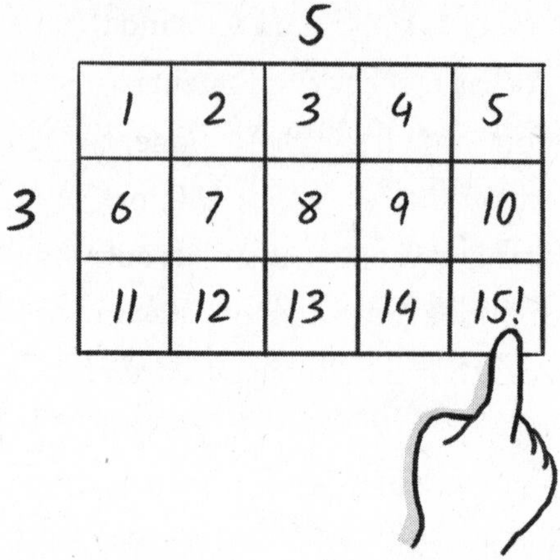

I don't know why it floored me, but I remember staring at our sketches completely gobsmacked. You could multiply one side length by the other and then know what was inside? The universe made sense. One side length of 3 inches multiplied by the other side length of 5 inches gave you 15 square inches. It was perfect.

The writer Alec Wilkinson wrote one of the most beautiful pieces on math that I have ever read, describing how he had not succeeded in the subject as a child, and then came back to it in his sixties and found its beauty. This is my favorite excerpt: "Mathematics is one of the most efficient means of approaching the great secret, of considering what lies past all that we can see or presently imagine. Mathematics doesn't describe the secret so much as it implies that there is one."

When my dad showed me how multiplication related to the real world by calculating area while I ate a personal pan pizza, I felt exactly that. There were secrets to the universe, and math was a way to see and understand them.

There were other revelatory moments—contemplating the world laid out on a coordinate plane, the perfect way that angles keep adding up to 90, 180, or 360 degrees in geometry—but the next one that stands out was in twelfth-grade calculus. While there are debates on whether and when to teach calculus, I hope my children take it no matter what profession they pursue, because it is a marvel of human ingenuity, a lucid and clear way to think. For me, it was even more than that. It represented a brush with divinity. Again: awe. Awe is our emotional response when we are in the presence of something vast that challenges our understanding of the world, like looking up at millions of stars in the night sky or marveling at the birth of a child.

I was lucky enough to take calculus at the same time I was in a physics course. The latter helped transform the abstract symbols into a mathematical explanation of a real problem I was considering, the relationship between velocity and acceleration. Velocity means speed and direction. Acceleration is the rate of change of speed. So, if you are in a car, your velocity might be 60 mph headed west. Your acceleration might be zero because you remain at 60 mph, or your acceleration may change because your car has sped up to 70 mph in one minute.

A lot of cool math exists to explain exactly what is happening in that car. Calculus is the math discipline needed to describe perfectly the motion of objects on Earth. In twelfth grade, calculus filled me with wonder. Was calculus invented, or was it discovered? We didn't invent motion. We didn't create gravity. So, how could we have invented the math that so elegantly explains it?

It left me with a big question. As Wilkinson says, "Where do numbers come from? No one knows. Were they invented by human beings? Hard to say. They appear to be embedded in the world in ways that we can't completely comprehend."

Ancient religions and cultures believed in the divinity of numbers, too. We can dismiss this as superstition or assume we are more sophisticated today, but if you approach these beliefs with an open mind, and an awareness of the possibilities of math, you'll discover something of value. In the Hindu tradition I come from, 108 is a sacred number. There are 108 prayer beads on a *japa mala*, a prayer bead necklace. The devotee is supposed to hold each bead and say a mantra, and complete the necklace by saying the mantra 108 times. You are told that if you can't complete 108, 54 or even 27 are okay because they are factors of 108. But doing a random number is not okay.

Always assuming it was superstition, I once built up the courage (in my forties, by the way) to ask a Hindu scholar why 108? It was an arbitrary number to me.

The answer I got from this learned Vedic scholar floored me. I frankly didn't believe it. I spent hours researching the answer, even doing the math myself to confirm it. What she told me was that ancient Hindu scholars had approximated that the distance between Earth and the moon, and the distance between Earth and the sun, were both a multiple of 108. According to their calculations, Earth was 108 moons away from the moon, and Earth was 108 suns away from the sun. Because the relationship to both celestial bodies embedded 108, they determined that the number was divine.

Doing some division to verify the math of the ancient Hindus, we see they were accurate despite their lack of modern measuring instruments. The average distance between Earth and the moon is about 238,855 miles. If you divide that by the diameter of the moon, which is 2,159 miles, you get a value of about 110. The distance from Earth to the sun is 93 million miles. If you divide this by the diameter of the sun, which is 864,938 miles, you get a value of 107.5.

You probably know $a^2 + b^2 = c^2$ as the Pythagorean theorem. We have records that this relationship was discovered, discussed, and obsessed over by many ancient civilizations. Knowledge of the theorem is first found in ancient Babylonian tablets thought to be dated to 1900–1600 BCE. Pythagoras came a thousand years later, around 500 BCE! It is also found in the Salba-Sutra text from India, which was written between 800 and 400 BCE. In the third century AD, Liu Hui, a Chinese scholar, reflected on it.

It's as if the ancients were looking for—and finding—the numerical secrets of the universe. They weren't inventing or creating math; they were discovering it.

I share these examples of the mystery and magnificence of numbers because I hope we aim as high as the ancients. In my decade-plus journey through the world of math teaching and learning, and in examining the deep data on our learning platform, I have ultimately learned one thing: Math is not only everywhere, math is for everyone. All kids can succeed in math. In fact, we can all succeed in math. We could, and should, love math. It's time that the adults get together and make that happen.

EPILOGUE

For the Love of Math

I HAVE USED THE WORDS *LOVE* AND *MATH* IN CON-junction many times in this book. As you may have guessed, I did that on purpose. I didn't do that to be provocative or to make you feel good, and I certainly didn't want you to dismiss me or my words.

I use the word *love* because I mean love.

What is love as it pertains to learning generally or learning math? The exploration of this question is a philosophical and theological discussion that stretches across millennia. There are synonyms I can offer for the love I am talking about. There are other words and expressions in teaching and learning that mean the same thing. They also require the same explanations—such as thirst for knowledge, burning with curiosity, passion for learning, and desire to know. Examine these words for a moment—*thirst, burning, passion, desire*; these are words of love. The love I am talking about is a change in you, in all of us; the change requires just a bit of patience, but it is worth it.

There is the mean, callous, and exclusive world of math. It discriminates and saps our collective potential. It's real; you didn't imagine it. Even with all my privileges, I have lived at the edges of it most of my life. It has broken me, hardened me, and then I have been reborn to loving math more than once. I wrote this book to acknowledge that and suggest that we should band together and reject it for all kids and for ourselves. Some trials in life are worth it, but the harshness pervasive in the world of learning math is not. We lose far more than we gain collectively. We should abandon it right now.

There is also the "tiger parent" world of math, one of fear, where a competition of who can endure the most suffering is actually the real game. In that game, we implicitly teach there is no love to be had for math, that success in math is a grind. That math is a grind. I mean "tiger parents" with no disrespect whatsoever. As the child of Indian immigrants, I know what it is like to grow up with the constant stress of giving up everything for possibility and arriving in a country with no backup plan. I was a lucky child because despite that stress, my parents loved math, learning, and knowledge generally.

But even if we break down the barriers, there is another exclusive world of math that we have to contend with. It is exclusive only until you decide to make a change in yourself, until you decide to see and love the beauty of math.

Once you do, math becomes far more inclusive, and here's the best part: Once you find that love, no one can take it from you.

In the first few weeks of kindergarten for my twin sons, during our morning walk to school, one of my boys would get nervous and upset. His little hand would grip my hand so tightly that I could sense his panic as physical electric shocks. His twin brother, happy and oblivious to this situation on the other side of my body, would release my right hand, smile at us, and run into school. But he would hold on tighter and tighter. His hand would finally go limp, likely because his muscles had given out, and then he would cry huge, silent tears. A teacher would come over to us silently, making meaningful eye contact with me, and gently guide him into the building. I would put on a strong face for him and her, but then also cry once they were out of sight. At the very top on the list of things I am most grateful for in my life are the schools my children have gone to and the educators who have taught them. The head of their elementary school, a legendary educator who recently passed away, rapidly developed a plan for my crying son that included fun, secret messages in the hallways, and special notes just for him at drop-off. Thanks to her hard work and knowledge of what true love is in learning, within a week or two, he was running into the school building. This same five-year-old boy would now wriggle free of my hand as the school building came into sight and, certainly, before I was ready. Then he'd terrify me as he sprinted down a full New York

City block into school. I would run after him with his twin brother in tow, trying to give him his backpack and a hug before he disappeared into the building.

That is the love I am talking about. After a few weeks of concerted effort on the part of educators, family, and most important, yourself, running as fast as you can into the school building while your mother is chasing you and pleading for you to slow down. A thirst for knowledge. Burning with curiosity. A passion for learning. The desire to know. And this is what I mean when I say we can all love learning math.

Nineteenth-century philosopher Søren Kierkegaard makes a distinction between spontaneous love and true love, urging us to seek the latter. Today, we often engage with math with a spontaneous love, a whimsical feeling that comes and goes. Spontaneous love happens to you; you don't decide or have any control. Kierkegaard describes it this way: "Spontaneous love can be changed within itself: it can be changed to its opposite, to hate. Hate is a love which has become its opposite, a ruined love." That is the reason why we hate math instead of feeling indifferent to it, because we are holding on to a ruined love. Remarkably, Kierkegaard goes on to provide an incisive description of anxiety, which so many of us feel when it comes to math: "Anxiously tortured by preoccupation with itself, it dares neither absolutely trust the beloved nor wholeheartedly surrender itself, lest it give too much and thereby continually burn itself as one burns himself on that which is not burning–except in the contact of anxiety." That's why we have math anxiety rather than math indifference.

The change in you is to approach math with more patience and with the knowledge that in math and in other fields of knowledge, true love is waiting. After all, anything worthwhile takes time and requires cultivation. It also requires the change in you that I referenced. The change in you is to be patient, calm, and seek that love. As Kierkegaard says, "True love, which has undergone the transformation of the eternal by becoming duty, is never changed, it has integrity." I think what Kierkegaard means is that the aim is to run into the school building; to experience burning curiosity is our true state. But what he shares is that it takes time and effort, a change in you, to cultivate that love. Further, unexpectedly, because there is so much hate and anxiety for math, we can have great hope. Their presence means the foundation of love, a "ruined love," can be built on. The "ruined love" is immature and with a change in you, it can be cultivated into true love for math.

Now get on with it. Give math another chance. Resuscitate your curiosity. Move past your ego, surrender, and be fearless. Go work hard on helping everyone, especially kids, *and* including yourself, love learning math.

Acknowledgments

I turned to many people for help with this book. First and foremost, I have learned so much from the teachers who use Zearn Math. I thank you all from the bottom of my heart. These teachers have shaped Zearn and my understanding of teaching and learning math. Second, I have gained insights through my conversations with elementary school teachers, middle school math teachers, school leaders, district and state administrators, parents, nonprofit executives, foundation leaders, policymakers, and STEM professionals over the last decade. Third, I have benefited greatly from many conversations with children primarily in the age range of three to thirteen. Without all these interactions, I could never have written this book.

I want to especially thank the Zearn team and board, past and present. I have never been a part of a team more capable, committed, kind, and fun. I could scarcely have imagined that such a team could come to be. I also want to thank the visionary Zearn cofounders for their courage and commitment and for including me on the ride of my life. Everything else insightful in this book came from our work together creating, building, and scaling Zearn Math.

I want to thank advisers and friends who rolled up their sleeves to help me bring this book to life. I'd like to thank Esmond Harmsworth, my agent, for his genuine encouragement and sage advice every step of the way. I am so grateful to my editors at Avery Penguin Random House, Nina Shield and Hannah Steigmeyer, for their belief and editorial skill.

I thank my family and friends, especially my parents and brother, for their support and understanding as I disappeared into this book. I also want to thank my wonderful nieces and nephews for their interesting and incisive questions and observations. Finally, I am filled with gratitude for my middle school twin boys and my husband and best friend, who helped, consoled, endured, and rejoiced with me through all the highs and lows of writing this book.

Finally, the book is entirely my responsibility, and thus the flaws are my doing. For those, I ask for your direct and constructive feedback, and I offer that making mistakes is how you learn. I hope to keep learning and getting better.

Notes

CHAPTER 1—WE ALL COULD HAVE BEEN MATH KIDS

1. **"what little we do know is highly contested":** Jay Caspian Kang, "What Do We Really Know about Teaching Kids Math?," *New Yorker,* November 18, 2022, https://www.newyorker.com/news/our-columnists/what-do-we-really-know-about-teaching-kids-math.

3. **the American high school revolution:** Claudia Goldin and Lawrence F. Katz, *The Race between Education and Technology* (Cambridge, MA: Belknap Press, 2010).

3. **fewer than 7 percent:** Goldin and Katz, *The Race between Education and Technology.*

3. **more than tenfold to over 70 percent:** Goldin and Katz, *The Race between Education and Technology.*

4. **"a great equalizer":** Roslin Growe and Paula S. Montgomery, "Educational Equity in America: Is Education the Great Equalizer?," *Professional Educator* 25, no. 2 (2003): 23–29.

5. **as India won its independence:** Guneeta Bhalla, "The Story of the 1947 Partition as Told by the People Who Were There,"

Humanities 43, no. 3 (Summer 2022), https://www.neh.gov/article/story-1947-partition-told-people-who-were-there.

6. **the book *Switch*:** Chip and Dan Heath, *Switch: How to Change Things When Change Is Hard,* 1st ed. (New York: Broadway Books, 2010).

10. **particular question, we failed:** "The Nation's Report Card | NAEP," National Assessment of Educational Progress, National Center for Education Statistics, accessed July 20, 2023, https://nces.ed.gov/nationsreportcard/.

12. **story of a little boy named Tanner:** Amanda Grennell, "A Child Lost a Sixth of His Brain, Then Made an Amazing Comeback," PBS *NewsHour,* August 2, 2018, https://www.pbs.org/newshour/science/this-child-lost-a-sixth-of-his-brain-the-rest-learned-to-pick-up-the-slack.

12. **London cab drivers:** Ferris Jabr, "Cache Cab: Taxi Drivers' Brains Grow to Navigate London's Streets," *Scientific American,* December 8, 2011, https://www.scientificamerican.com/article/london-taxi-memory/.

13. **Jean Piaget, the child development expert:** Jean Piaget, "Part I: Cognitive Development in Children: Piaget Development and Learning," *Journal of Research in Science Teaching* 2, no. 3 (1964): 176–86, https://doi.org/10.1002/tea.3660020306.

13. **the preschoolers won:** Alice Park, "Preschooler's Innate Knowledge Means They Can Probably Do Algebra," *Time,* March 20, 2014, https://time.com/28952/preschoolers-innate-knowledge-means-they-can-probably-do-algebra/.

14. **Pigeons not only can count:** James Gorman, "How Smart Is This Bird? Let It Count the Ways," *New York Times,* December 22, 2011, sec. Science, https://www.nytimes

.com/2011/12/23/science/pigeons-can-learn-higher-math -as-well-as-monkeys-study-suggests.html.

14. **Primates can rank items on a screen:** Jordana Cepelewicz, "Animals Can Count and Use Zero. How Far Does Their Number Sense Go?," *Quanta Magazine*, August 9, 2021, https://www.quantamagazine.org/animals-can-count-and -use-zero-how-far-does-their-number-sense-go-20210809/.

16. **the line in this chart:** "Literate and Illiterate World Population," Our World in Data, https://ourworldindata.org/grapher/ literate-and-illiterate-world-population.

17. **Program for International Student Assessment:** OECD, *PISA 2022 Results (Volume I): The State of Learning and Equity in Education* (Paris: OECD Publishing, 2023), https://doi .org/10.1787/53f23881-en.

PART I: THE MYTHS

21. **the night sky on the Fourth of July:** Benedict Carey, "What Your Brain Looks Like When It Solves a Math Problem," *New York Times*, July 28, 2016, sec. Science, https://www .nytimes.com/2016/07/29/science/brain-scans-math .html.

21. **93 percent of Americans feel some degree of math anxiety:** Anya Kamenetz and Cory Turner, "Math Anxiety Is Real. Here's How to Help Your Child Avoid It," KQED, September 8, 2020, https://www.kqed.org /mindshift/56637/math-anxiety-is-real-heres-how-to-help -your-child-avoid-it.

21. **In a survey of US teachers:** Sarah D. Sparks, "The Myth Fueling Math Anxiety," *Education Week*, January 7, 2020, sec. Teaching & Learning, Curriculum, https://www

.edweek.org/teaching-learning/the-myth-fueling-math-anxiety/2020/01.

21. **high school students reported feeling "helpless":** Kamenetz and Turner, "Math Anxiety Is Real. Here's How to Help Your Child Avoid It."

21. **"People who are highly math anxious avoid math":** Mark H. Ashcraft and Jeremy A. Krause, "Working Memory, Math Performance, and Math Anxiety," *Psychonomic Bulletin & Review* 14, no. 2 (April 1, 2007): 243–48, https://doi.org/10.3758/BF03194059.

22. **sacrifice accuracy for speed:** Richard J. Daker et al., "First-Year Students' Math Anxiety Predicts STEM Avoidance and Underperformance throughout University, Independently of Math Ability," *Npj Science of Learning* 6, no. 1 (June 14, 2021): 1–13, https://doi.org/10.1038/s41539-021-00095-7.

22. **four out of five students:** Sparks, "The Myth Fueling Math Anxiety."

CHAPTER 2—SPEED ISN'T EVERYTHING

26. **120 million Apollo-era spacecrafts:** Alexis C. Madrigal, "Your Smart Toaster Can't Hold a Candle to the Apollo Computer," *Atlantic*, July 16, 2019, https://www.theatlantic.com/science/archive/2019/07/underappreciated-power-apollo-computer/594121/.

27. **physics problems to solve under time pressure:** Sian Beilock, *Choke* (New York: Atria Books, 2011), https://www.simonandschuster.com/books/Choke/Sian-Beilock/9781416596189.

29. **Jim Stigler, a legendary researcher:** Alix Spiegel, "Struggle for Smarts? How Eastern and Western Cultures Tackle Learning,"

NPR *Morning Edition*, accessed July 20, 2023, https://www.npr.org/sections/health-shots/2012/11/12/164793058/struggle-for-smarts-how-eastern-and-western-cultures-tackle-learning.

29. **"regular, timed activities to build up fluency":** "Assisting Students Struggling with Mathematics: Intervention in the Elementary Grades," IES, What Works Clearinghouse, March 2021, https://ies.ed.gov/ncee/wwc/PracticeGuide/26.

30. **American philosopher William James:** William James, *The Principles of Psychology* (New York: Cosimo, 2007).

30. **we now term working memory:** Nathan S. Rose et al., "Similarities and Differences between Working Memory and Long-Term Memory: Evidence from the Levels-of-Processing Span Task," *Journal of Experimental Psychology: Learning, Memory, and Cognition* 36, no. 2 (2010): 471–83, https://doi.org/10.1037/a0018405.

31. **a man named H.M.:** NPR Staff, "The Lobotomy of Patient H.M: A Personal Tragedy and Scientific Breakthrough," NPR, August 14, 2016, sec. Author Interviews, https://www.npr.org/2016/08/14/489997276/how-patient-h-m-and-his-lobotomy-contributed-to-understanding-memories.

33. **the James Webb Space Telescope:** "James Webb Space Telescope," NASA Solar System Exploration, accessed July 20, 2023, https://solarsystem.nasa.gov/missions/james-webb-space-telescope/in-depth.

35. **traced back to the math wars:** Alan H. Schoenfeld, "The Math Wars," *Educational Policy* 18, no. 1 (January 1, 2004): 253–86, https://doi.org/10.1177/0895904803260042.

36. **In 2008, the National Mathematics Advisory Panel:** National Mathematics Advisory Panel, "Foundations for Success: The Final Report of the National Mathematics Advisory Panel" (Washington, DC: U.S. Department of Education, March 2008), https://files.eric.ed.gov/fulltext/ED500486.pdf.

37. **William Heard Kilpatrick:** Jay Caspian Kang, "How Math Became an Object of the Culture Wars," *New Yorker*, November 15, 2022, https://www.newyorker.com/news/our-columnists/how-math-became-an-object-of-the-culture-wars.

37. **David Snedden, a Columbia:** Diane Polachek, "Planning Instruction in Mathematics at the Early Childhood and Elementary School Levels," LinkedIn, May 24, 2022, https://www.linkedin.com/pulse/planning-instruction-mathematics-early-childhood-school-polachek.

38. **57 percent in 1909 to less than 25 percent by 1955:** "America's Maths Wars," *Economist*, November 6, 2021, https://www.economist.com/united-states/2021/11/06/americas-maths-wars.

44. **student perception of the ability:** Aneeta Rattan, Catherine Good, and Carol S. Dweck, " 'It's Ok—Not Everyone Can Be Good at Math': Instructors with an Entity Theory Comfort (and Demotivate) Students," *Journal of Experimental Social Psychology* 48, no. 3 (May 1, 2012): 731–37, https://doi.org/10.1016/j.jesp.2011.12.012.

CHAPTER 3—TRICKS ARE NOT THE ANSWER

48. **Numeracy is innate:** Jordana Cepelewicz, "Animals Can Count and Use Zero. How Far Does Their Number Sense Go?," *Quanta Magazine*, August 9, 2021, https://www

.quantamagazine.org/animals-can-count-and-use-zero-how-far-does-their-number-sense-go-20210809.

51. **"the lamest sing-along ever":** Ben Orlin, "When Memorization Gets in the Way of Learning," *Atlantic,* September 10, 2013, https://www.theatlantic.com/education/archive/2013/09/when-memorization-gets-in-the-way-of-learning/279425/.

52. **better at congruent memory making:** Marlieke T. R. van Kesteren et al., "Differential Roles for Medial Prefrontal and Medial Temporal Cortices in Schema-Dependent Encoding: From Congruent to Incongruent," special issue, *Neuropsychologia* 51, no. 12 (October 1, 2013): 2352–59, https://doi.org/10.1016/j.neuropsychologia.2013.05.027.

61. **Muhammad ibn Musa al-Khwarizmi:** David M. Nabirahni, Brian R. Evans, and Ashley Persaud, "Al-Khwarizmi (Algorithm) and the Development of Algebra," *Mathematics Teaching Research Journal* 11, no. 1 (2019).

CHAPTER 4—THERE IS NO SINGLE WAY

69. **300 BCE shouting "Eureka!":** Rachel Ross, "Eureka! The Archimedes Principle," Live Science, April 25, 2017, https://www.livescience.com/58839-archimedes-principle.html.

74. **consider some downtime:** Ferris Jabr, "Why Your Brain Needs More Downtime," *Scientific American,* October 15, 2013, https://www.scientificamerican.com/article/mental-downtime/.

76. **professor Mriganka Sur:** "MIT Research—Brain Processing of Visual Information," *MIT News,* December 19, 1996, https://news.mit.edu/1996/visualprocessing.

76. **David Knill, also a professor:** Susan Hagen, "The Mind's Eye," *Rochester Review* 74, no. 4 (March 2012): 32–37.

CHAPTER 5—KNOW YOU BELONG

87. **students with the highest working memory:** Craig Barton, *How I Wish I'd Taught Maths: Lessons Learned from Research, Conversations with Experts, and 12 Years of Mistakes* (York, PA: Learning Sciences International, 2018).

88. **referenced this as *churn*:** Claude Steele, "Churn: Life in the Increasingly Diverse World of Higher Education and How to Make It Work," Faculty Advancement Network, February 4, 2022, https://www.facultyadvancementnetwork.org/claude-steele-churn-life-in-the-increasingly-diverse-world-of-higher-education-and-how-to-make-it-work.

96. **in 2005 when Larry Summers:** Daniel J. Hemel, "Summers' Comments on Women and Science Draw Ire," *Harvard Crimson*, January 14, 2005, https://www.thecrimson.com/article/2005/1/14/summers-comments-on-women-and-science/.

96. **STEM pipeline is sometimes called "leaky":** Linda Calhoun, Shruthi Jayaram, and Natasha Madorsky, "Leaky Pipelines or Broken Scaffolding? Supporting Women's Leadership in STEM (SSIR)," *Stanford Social Innovation Review*, June 1, 2022, https://ssir.org/articles/entry/leaky_pipelines_or_broken_scaffolding_supporting_womens_leadership_in_stem.

96. **Carol Dweck, Aneeta Rattan, and Catherine Good:** Catherine Good, Aneeta Rattan, and Carol S. Dweck, "Why Do Women Opt Out? Sense of Belonging and Women's Representation in Mathematics," *Journal of Personality and*

Social Psychology 102, no. 4 (2012): 700–717, https://doi.org/10.1037/a0026659.

98. **"Am I the kind of person who":** Michael Broda et al., "Reducing Inequality in Academic Success for Incoming College Students: A Randomized Trial of Growth Mindset and Belonging Interventions," *Journal of Research on Educational Effectiveness* 11, no. 3 (July 3, 2018): 317–38, https://doi.org/10.1080/19345747.2018.1429037.

99. **start with growth mindset:** Carol Dweck, "What Having a 'Growth Mindset' Actually Means," *Harvard Business Review*, January 13, 2016, https://hbr.org/2016/01/what-having-a-growth-mindset-actually-means.

102. **they were reminded they were outsiders:** Claude M. Steele, "A Threat in the Air: How Stereotypes Shape Intellectual Identity and Performance," *American Psychologist* 52, no. 6 (1997): 613–29, https://doi.org/10.1037/0003-066X.52.6.613.

CHAPTER 6—USE PICTURES AND OBJECTS

111. **A&W's Third Pounder:** "The Truth about A&W's Third-Pound Burger and the Major Math Mix-Up," A&W, accessed July 20, 2023, https://awrestaurants.com/blog/aw-third-pound-burger-fractions.

113. **"And we failed.":** Elizabeth Green, "Why Do Americans Stink at Math?," *New York Times*, July 23, 2014, sec. Magazine, https://www.nytimes.com/2014/07/27/magazine/why-do-americans-stink-at-math.html.

114. **such as Finland:** "Education GPS—Finland," OECD, accessed July 20, 2023, https://gpseducation.oecd.org/CountryProfile?primaryCountry=FIN&treshold=10&topic=PI.

114. **and Singapore—were able:** Jeevan Vasagar, "Why Singapore's Kids Are So Good at Maths," *Financial Times*, July 22, 2016, sec. FT Magazine, https://www.ft.com/content/2e4c61f2-4ec8-11e6-8172-e39ecd3b86fc.

114. **attach your learning:** Daniel T. Willingham, "How Knowledge Helps," *American Federation of Teachers* 30, no. 1 (Spring 2006), https://www.aft.org/ae/spring2006/willingham; Marlieke T. R. van Kesteren et al., "Differential Roles for Medial Prefrontal and Medial Temporal Cortices in Schema-Dependent Encoding: From Congruent to Incongruent," special issue, *Neuropsychologia* 51, no. 12 (October 1, 2013): 2352–59, https://doi.org/10.1016/j.neuropsychologia.2013.05.027.

119. **learning deepens when we can use multiple modalities:** Margarete Delazer et al., "Learning by Strategies and Learning by Drill—Evidence from an fMRI Study," *NeuroImage* 25, no. 3 (April 15, 2005): 838–49, https://doi.org/10.1016/j.neuroimage.2004.12.009.

121. **thinking in symbols:** Andreas Nieder, "Prefrontal Cortex and the Evolution of Symbolic Reference," special issue, *Current Opinion in Neurobiology* 19, no. 1 (February 1, 2009): 99–108, https://doi.org/10.1016/j.conb.2009.04.008.

122. **showed a two-and-a-half-year-old girl a dollhouse:** Judy S. DeLoache, Kevin F. Miller, and Karl S. Rosengren, "The Credible Shrinking Room: Very Young Children's Performance with Symbolic and Nonsymbolic Relations," *Psychological Science* 8, no. 4 (July 1, 1997): 308–13, https://doi.org/10.1111/j.1467-9280.1997.tb00443.x.

123. **experimentalists include Maria Montessori:** "Who Was Maria Montessori?," American Montessori Society, accessed July 20, 2023, https://amshq.org/About-Montessori/History-of-Montessori/Who-Was-Maria-Montessori.

124. **As Bruner noted:** Jerome S. Bruner, *The Process of Education*, rev. ed. (Cambridge, MA: Harvard University Press, 1977), 33, https://doi.org/10.2307/j.ctvk12qst.

124. **where "Singapore Math":** John Hoven and Barry Garelick, "Singapore Math: Simple or Complex?," *Educational Leadership* 65 (November 1, 2007).

CHAPTER 7—MAKE AN EASIER PROBLEM

140. **"2,000 ways not to make a lightbulb":** Megan Jackson, "Learn to Embrace the Art of Failure," *theNEWS*, June 24, 2019, https://www.achrnews.com/articles/141466-learn-to-embrace-the-art-of-failure.

CHAPTER 8—TRY A DIFFERENT WAY

143. ***Zen and the Art of Motorcycle Maintenance*:** Robert M. Pirsig, *Zen and the Art of Motorcycle Maintenance: An Inquiry into Values* (New York: Morrow, 1974), 166, http://catdir.loc.gov/catdir/enhancements/fy0911/73012275-b.html.

149. **called Spelling Bee:** "Play Spelling Bee," *New York Times*, sec. Games, accessed July 20, 2023, https://www.nytimes.com/puzzles/spelling-bee.

154. **famed cognitive scientist Daniel Willingham:** Daniel T. Willingham, "How to Get Your Mind to Read," *New York Times*, November 25, 2017, sec. Opinion, https://www.nytimes.com/2017/11/25/opinion/sunday/how-to-get-your-mind-to-read.html.

CHAPTER 9—PRACTICE WITH PURPOSE

166. **he burned every sketch in his studio:** Allison McNearney, "The Mystery of Why Michelangelo Burned His Sketches Just Before He Died," *Daily Beast*, April 21, 2019, sec. Arts and Culture, https://www.thedailybeast.com/the-mystery-of-why-michelangelo-burned-his-sketches-just-before-he-died.

166. **the leaky STEM pipeline:** Doug Lederman, "Who Changes Majors? (Not Who You Think)," *Inside Higher Ed*, December 7, 2017, https://www.insidehighered.com/news/2017/12/08/nearly-third-students-change-major-within-three-years-math-majors-most.

166. **significantly higher for women and Black and Latino students:** National Academy of Engineering and National Research Council, "Chapter 3: The Loss of Students from STEM Majors," in *Community Colleges in the Evolving STEM Education Landscape: Summary of a Summit* (Washington, DC: National Academies Press, 2012), 19–22, https://doi.org/10.17226/13399.

167. **One study conducted by Penn State University:** Danfei Hu et al., "Not All Scientists Are Equal: Role Aspirants Influence Role Modeling Outcomes in STEM," *Basic and Applied Social Psychology* 42, no. 3 (March 6, 2020): 192–208, https://doi.org/10.1080/01973533.2020.1734006.

167. **"a genius's predestined success story":** Pennsylvania State University, "Sorry, Einstein: Hard Workers May Make Better Role Models than Geniuses," PhysOrg, March 11, 2020, https://phys.org/news/2020-03-einstein-hard-workers-role-geniuses.html.

168. **calls it deliberate practice:** K. Anders Ericsson, Ralf T. Krampe, and Clemens Tesch-Römer, "The Role

of Deliberate Practice in the Acquisition of Expert Performance," *Psychological Review* 100, no. 3 (1993): 363–406, https://doi.org/10.1037/0033-295X.100.3.363.

168. **In his book *Peak*:** Anders Ericsson and Robert Pool, *Peak: Secrets from the New Science of Expertise* (New York: HarperCollins, 2016).

168. **10,000 hours of practice is required to achieve expertise:** Malcolm Gladwell, *Outliers: The Story of Success* (New York: Penguin Books, 2009).

168. **Daniel Willingham, who translates:** Daniel Willingham, "Ask the Cognitive Scientist: What Will Improve a Student's Memory?," *American Educator* 32, no. 4 (2013): 17–25.

181. **students who struggle the most show the most gains:** Zearn Math Efficacy Research, *Students across Subgroups and Math Proficiency Levels Who Consistently Used Zearn Math Grew an Average of 1.3 Grade Levels in One Year of Learning* (Zearn, 2023), https://about.zearn.org/insights/zearn-impact-large-southern-district.

CHAPTER 10—THE EQUATION THAT WILL DECIDE OUR FATE

185. **career aspirations of young people:** Sarah D. Sparks, "Students' 'Dream Jobs' Out of Sync with Emerging Economy," *Education Week*, January 22, 2020, sec. Teaching & Learning, College & Workforce Readiness, https://www.edweek.org/teaching-learning/students-dream-jobs-out-of-sync-with-emerging-economy/2020/01.

186. **In 1980, about half of those employed:** *The State of American Jobs* (Pew Research Center, October 6, 2016), https://www.pewresearch.org/social-trends/2016/10/06/the-state-of-american-jobs/.

186. **the top six skills employers are looking for:** Ashley Finley, *How College Contributes to Workforce Success: Employer Views on What Matters Most* (AAC&U, 2021), https://www.aacu.org/research/how-college-contributes-to-workforce-success.

188. **the famous Lascaux:** "The Cave Art Paintings of the Lascaux Cave," Bradshaw Foundation, 2003, https://www.bradshawfoundation.com/lascaux/.

188. **LIDAR (light detection and ranging):** *Daily Chela* Staff, "Archaeologists Discover Sprawling Maya City," *The Daily Chela* (blog), January 31, 2023, https://www.dailychela.com/archaeologists-discover-sprawling-maya-city/.

188. **STEM heavy at 23 percent:** Abigail Okrent and Amy Burke, "The STEM Labor Force of Today: Scientists, Engineers, and Skilled Technical Workers," *Science and Engineering Indicators* (August 2021), https://ncses.nsf.gov/pubs/nsb20212.

188. **two million people with computer science degrees:** Data USA and Deloitte, "Computer Science," Data USA, 2021, https://datausa.io/profile/cip/computer-science-110701.

188. **higher salaries and lower unemployment rates:** Amy Burke, Abigail Okrent, and Katherine Hale, "The State of U.S. Science and Engineering 2022," *Science and Engineering Indicators* (January 18, 2022), https://ncses.nsf.gov/pubs/nsb20221.

189. **nearly double the comparable median salary:** Brian Kennedy, Richard Fry, and Cary Funk, "6 Facts about America's STEM Workforce and Those Training for It," Pew Research Center, April 14, 2021, https://www.pewresearch.org/short-reads/2021/04/14/6-facts-about-americas-stem-workforce-and-those-training-for-it/.

189. **four out of five children who fail algebra drop out:** Bill Gates, "More Students Flunk This High School Course than Any

Other," *GatesNotes* (blog), December 7, 2021, https://www.gatesnotes.com/Helping-students-succeed-in-Algebra.

189. **One recent study:** Adam Hardy, "The Wage Gap between College and High School Grads Just Hit a Record High," *Money,* February 14, 2022, https://money.com/wage-gap-college-high-school-grads/.

189. **a study titled *Math Matters*:** Heather Rose and Julian R. Betts, *Math Matters: The Links between High School Curriculum, College Graduation, and Earnings* (San Francisco: Public Policy Institute of California, 2001).

190. **The NAEP had shown:** Erin Richards, "Despite Common Core and More Testing, Reading and Math Scores Haven't Budged in a Decade," *USA Today,* October 30, 2019, https://www.usatoday.com/story/news/education/2019/10/29/national-math-reading-level-test-score-common-core-standards-phonics/2499622001/.

190. **nearly 50 percent of students who pursued a STEM degree:** Peg Tyre, "The Math Revolution," *Atlantic,* February 9, 2016, https://www.theatlantic.com/magazine/archive/2016/03/the-math-revolution/426855/.

190. **temporary visa holders:** National Center for Science and Engineering Statistics, *2020 Doctorate Recipients from U.S. Universities* (National Science Foundation, 2021) https://ncses.nsf.gov/pubs/nsf22300/report/temporary-visa-holder-plans.

192. **Consider the 2007–08 financial crisis:** Ylan Q. Mui, "Americans Saw Wealth Plummet 40 Percent from 2007 to 2010, Federal Reserve Says," *Washington Post,* May 20, 2023, https://www.washingtonpost.com/business/economy

/fed-americans-wealth-dropped-40-percent/2012/06/11 /gJQAlIsCVV_story.html.

194. **Bill Gates shares in his book:** Bill Gates, *How to Avoid a Climate Disaster: The Solutions We Have and the Breakthroughs We Need* (New York: Knopf Doubleday Publishing Group, 2021).

CHAPTER 11—TEACH OUR CHILDREN WELL

197. **stories of the "Mississippi miracle":** Marta W. Aldrich, "Tennessee Looks to 'Mississippi Miracle' as It Grapples with Stagnant Reading Scores," *Chalkbeat Tennessee*, February 23, 2023, https://tn.chalkbeat.org/2023/2/23/23611426/tennessee-reading-retention-mississippi-miracle-bill-lee-legislature.

197. ***Sold a Story*:** Emily Hanford, "How Teaching Kids to Read Went So Wrong," October 20, 2022, *Sold a Story*, produced by American Public Media, podcast, accessed July 27, 2023, https://features.apmreports.org/sold-a-story/.

199. **"Dealing drugs? That's impossible":** *The Simpsons*, season 21, episode 18, "Chief of Hearts," aired April 18, 2010, on Fox.

199. **a million-dollar prize:** Linda B. Glaser, "Physicist Offers New Take on Million-Dollar Math Problem," *Cornell Chronicle*, August 1, 2019, https://news.cornell.edu/stories/2019/08/physicist-offers-new-take-million-dollar-math-problem.

200. **classic *Peggy Sue Got Married*:** *Peggy Sue Got Married*, directed by Francis Ford Coppola (Culver City, CA: TriStar Pictures, 1986).

207. **Cornell University mathematician Steven Strogatz:** Steven D. Levitt, "Steven Strogatz Thinks You Don't Know What Math

Is," January 6, 2023, *People I (Mostly) Admire*, produced by Freakonomics, podcast, accessed July 27, 2023, https://freakonomics.com/podcast/steven-strogatz-thinks-you-dont-know-what-math-is/.

208. **345,000 third- to fifth-grade students:** Shalinee Sharma and Shirin Hashim, "Mindsets toward Math: Survey Finds High Zearn Math Usage Tied to More Positive Mindsets about Math," Zearn, 2018, https://about.zearn.org/research/mindsets-toward-math.

CHAPTER 12—FROM SORTING TO TEACHING

212. **99th percentile for a man:** PK, "Height Percentile Calculator by Gender (United States)," DQYDJ, 2016, https://dqydj.com/height-percentile-calculator-for-men-and-women.

214. **reaching proficiency in mathematics:** Sarah Mervosh and Ashley Wu, "Math Scores Fell in Nearly Every State, and Reading Dipped on National Exam," *New York Times*, October 24, 2022, sec. U.S., https://www.nytimes.com/2022/10/24/us/math-reading-scores-pandemic.html.

216. **move more slowly through problem-solving:** Sian Beilock, *Choke* (New York: Atria Books, 2011), https://www.simonandschuster.com/books/Choke/Sian-Beilock/9781416596189.

228. **"the great secret":** Alec Wilkinson, "Math Is the Great Secret," *New York Times*, September 18, 2022, sec. Opinion, https://www.nytimes.com/2022/09/18/opinion/math-adolescence-mystery.html.

230. **"Where do numbers come from?":** Wilkinson, "Math Is the Great Secret."

231. the Pythagorean theorem: *Encyclopaedia Britannica Online*, s.v. "Pythagorean Theorem," accessed July 8, 2023, https://www.britannica.com/science/Pythagorean-theorem.

EPILOGUE: FOR THE LOVE OF MATH

236. "its opposite, a ruined love": Soren Kierkegaard, *Works of Love*, trans. Howard Hong and Edna Hong (New York: Harper Perennial Modern Thought, 2009), 49.

236. burn itself as one burns himself: Kierkegaard, *Works of Love*, 50.

237. it has integrity: Kierkegaard, *Works of Love*, 49.

Index